How did you get to be here?
Stephen Sondheim:
Merrily We Roll Along (1981)

This 'Shower of Gold' scene; Act 3, scene 3, in Charles Kean's 1859 production of Henry V at the Empress Theatre; a scene which lasts less than one page in most printed editions, yet was staged here with two horses, and 140 performers including dancers with tambourines.
By F Lloyds. Reproduced with permission of V&A Images.

How did we get here from there?
Brian Freeland:
Searching for my Tambourine (2019)
part memoir; part theatre anthology.

Also by Brian Freeland:

Books
AROUND THE WORLD IN EIGHTY PLAYS
MEANDERINGS: A RIVER AND A LIFE

Stage Scripts
LETTERS FROM THE HEN HOUSE
YOUR NUMBER'S UP
SEE YOU IN HEAVEN
THE BEXHILL BUDGERIGAR
ROBINSON CRUSOE
HUMPTY DUMPTY
(with Christopher Rush)
A MERRY MEETING
WILL
A TWELVEMONTH AND A DAY
LILIES THAT FESTER

Stage Adaptations
AMY'S SPAGHETTI
(from a radio play by Colin Hough)
LAST LOVES
(from a radio play by Roni Robinson)

Screenplays
FRUITS DE MER
(from two short stories by Emile Zola)
SHAKESPEARE'S FAMILIES
(developed from WILL by Christopher Rush)

more details on www.brianfreeland.co.uk

SEARCHING FOR MY TAMBOURINE

by

BRIAN FREELAND

ATWP

British Library Cataloguing-in-Publication Data.
A catalogue for this book is available on request from the British Library.

ISBN: 978-0-9934431-7-6

SEARCHING FOR MY TAMBOURINE
is published by ATWP
and printed in the UK by
Scantech, Hastings TN35 4NR

CHAPTERS

INTRODUCTION

In the summer of 1966, shortly after England's football team had won the World Cup, I teamed up with theatre colleague David Sculpher to convert his ex-BBC Radio vehicle into a comfortable 'camper-van'. Together with a couple of young ladies we set out to drive across Europe: no particular route planned; no timetable. Florence and Venice, of course, and an unforgettable night of Opera in the Amphitheatre at Verona (*above*). Then down the full length of what was then Yugoslavia, heading for Greece. Visas required at the border, but few problems after that. Whenever we produced our football at the various Yugoslav camp sites we were quickly surrounded by youngsters eager to practice their fluent English; 'Bobbee Charlton; Bobbee Moore; Nobbee Stiles'.

Passing through the southern border controls into Greece we immediately discovered what we really should have known, that the Yugoslav dinar had no value outside of that country. We simply turned around, drove back through the border control to the nearest camp site, and blew the lot on an excellent meal and a few drinks. We also acquired a cat, but maybe more about that later.

Into Greece, and heading towards Athens, we stopped off at a little village fete. Nothing special: like village fetes anywhere in the world there were a few small fairground rides; an arena, and various stalls and sideshows. Except that, just near the entrance, this village fete had a man playing a tambourine. The man was not very tall; certainly not young, casually dressed, thinning hair; uncovered because his cap was on the ground in front of him. A cap filling with coins from an audience enjoying the performance of a man who sang a little, and danced a little, and smiled a lot, and played his tambourine as though he was entertaining the gods on Olympus. A man clearly at peace with the world.

David and I had each recently finished contracts with opera companies: David at Sadlers Wells; I with Scottish Opera. Our performances involved several pantechnicons crammed with scenery and costumes and lighting and musical instruments: a huge payroll of singers, musicians, administrators, wardrobe staff and technicians; overnight journeys from one city to another to large venues with up-to-date technical equipment, dressing rooms, staff, publicity and box office. All this merely to stage a musical entertainment. And yet here was an elderly man entertaining people, making a living, with just a tambourine and a cloth cap. I asked myself what could I do to that degree of self-contained professionalism? Was there no one ability in which I could challenge all competition; could touch an individual level of seeming perfection? Nothing apparently, although, understanding life backwards, I can point to that village fete experience as the start of a career spent subconsciously 'searching for my own tambourine'.

According to William Hazlitt (1778-1830) in his essay *On the Knowledge of Character* there is nothing that helps a man in his conduct through life more than a knowledge of his own characteristic weaknesses; and nothing tends more to the success of a man's talents than knowing the limits of his faculties, which he then concentrates on some practicable object. 'One man can do but one thing'.

'Universal pretensions end in nothing' he wrote. Hazlitt considered there were those who have, for want of this self-knowledge, gone strangely out of their way in their search for this *practical object*, and others who had never found it at all despite a lifetime of searching.

Hazlitt also observed that authors in general over-rate the extent and value of posthumous fame: a depressing thought for an author commencing a new book in his eighty-first year. Fortunately the book will have a happy ending: I did find my 'practical object'; *my tambourine*, admittedly rather late in life, and only after having gone *strangely out of my way* in far too many different directions and, indeed, in many different countries. That search is the 'clothes-line' on which I shall peg some memories (not all of them mine) of people and places, together with personal experiences from the past eighty years. My apologies in advance if you have come across some of these anecdotes in my previous publications, but their relevance to the theme of this, my final book, encouraged one last airing.

CHAPTER ONE
BEGINNERS ON STAGE, PLEASE.

In the late 1950s a new breed of playwrights, led by John Osborne, began to assert themselves at the Royal Court Theatre in London. Simultaneously, a new breed of actors emerged to interpret their work. One of the latter, a then largely-unknown Peter O'Toole, joined the Bristol Old Vic straight from RADA and played a series of leading parts which included Hamlet, Vladimir in *Waiting for* Godot, and Jimmy Porter in *Look Back in Anger*.

Tom Stoppard, then a twenty-year-old reporter for the Bristol Evening World, reviewed these productions and claims it was O'Toole's blazing performances which turned him onto theatre.

'By the end of that season' he wrote, 'I was incubating a new vocation'. Those same O'Toole performances also determined my own future career – although I should first have to complete my National Service in the RAF.

I was one of a small group of airmen studying Mandarin Chinese at a language school just outside Bristol. I had slight experience of theatre through amateur dramatics and school plays and, to break the monotony of wall-to-wall Mandarin, I sneaked into the city one evening with another amateur actor, aircraftsman Mick Brown, to see Bernard Shaw's play *Man and Superman* performed by the Bristol Old Vic in their stunningly-beautiful Theatre Royal.

Giving a *blazing performance* in the lead role of John Tanner was, indeed, Peter O'Toole. I was hooked right from the moment of his first entrance which seemed to begin at the stage door (some three floors below the Old Vic stage) and get louder and angrier until he finally burst through the doors upstage centre. Wow! What an entrance.

And that's where it all started. My future was decided that evening: I came out of the theatre knowing exactly what I wanted to do for the rest of my life. What I couldn't have foreseen then was that I would go on to work with Peter O'Toole, and with the play's director Denis Carey – both covered in later chapters. Mick and I saw most of Mr O'Toole's performances at the Bristol Old Vic that season including Vladimir in *Waiting For Godot*, *Mother Goose*, and Archangel Gabriel in *Sodom and Gomorrah*.

We also visited the Little Theatre under the roof of Bristol's Colston Hall, where the Rapier Players led by Robert Russell and Peggy Ann Wood presented top-quality fortnightly rep – beautiful staging and lighting, excellent performances – all mounted without any form of public subsidy.

At the end of our course the RAF flew us out to Hong Kong (on a BOAC Argonaut!) for a year, returning via Changi Airport at the end of 1958. In January 1959, barely three weeks after demob, I started my first theatre job – Trainee Manager with Moss Empires Ltd. There were Empire Theatres in most cities and larger towns throughout the country, and they also had three flagship venues in London; the Palladium, the Hippodrome and – my first theatre - the Victoria Palace. I had been appointed on the strength of my pre-National Service experience (three years as Junior Accounts Clerk in the Borough Treasurer's Department at Fulham Town Hall) and RSA Certificates in Book-keeping. I soon settled into the routines, but quickly realised that the job was a mistake: I had merely exchanged one office for another.

What had excited me on those visits to the Bristol Old Vic was the quality of the productions. I wanted to be involved with all that – not as an actor, I hasten to add: I don't dislike actors (well, a few perhaps) but I don't really understand them, and certainly never wanted to be one. Tom Stoppard's wonderful line in *Rosencrantz and Guildenstern Are Dead* – 'We're actors; we're the opposite of people!' - is too close to the truth. My interest was in getting a production from script to stage – involving, as I quickly appreciated, a disparate range of increasingly-technical crafts. I was already twenty-one: too late (and too poor) to go to drama school, so I quite deliberately took a series of short-term contracts getting experience in all the different back-stage departments – stage technician, lighting technician, lighting design and stage management. Theatre has become desperately more 'technical' since then, but even in 1959 there was a great deal to learn: three years of touring, summer seasons and resident productions provided much early helpful experience.

Putting on a show in Athens in 500BC in an amphitheatre surrounded by rows of stone benches, no scenery, no lights, must have been a doddle by comparison. In his book *Drama* Ashley Dukes wrote 'Drama in Greek signifies 'action', and the origin of drama lay in performance. Placing their performance space in the midst of the audience encouraged popular participation in that drama'.

The *producer* in the Greek amphitheatres was the *Archon*. He chose the plays and supervised the chorus by – says Mr Dukes – 'exercising the sternest discipline'. Pre-Equity days, obviously. Across the Adriatic, in the Roman theatres, the *producers* purchased plays from the poets, and performed them at their own charge.

In the Elizabethan theatre, with plays being written (or re-written) for a regular company on an open stage, the writer himself almost certainly had a hand in the production. It's worth remembering that up until this point, apart from command performances in palaces and stately homes, theatre had been performed in the open air, and in daylight. James Burbage assembled this Playhouse at Blackfriars (*right*), but his son Richard did not get a licence for it until 1609.

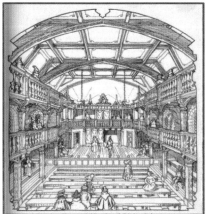

From that year the Kings Men performed at the Globe in summer, and indoors at Blackfriars in the winter by the flickering light of lanterns and candles. *The Tempest* was first seen indoors, at the Banqueting House in Whitehall as part of The Revels, and later at Blackfriars.

Theatre was banned during Cromwell's Republic, and was much-changed when it resumed in 1660 following the restoration of the monarchy. Ben Jonson's farces gave way to Restoration Comedies, many described as 'immoral, lacking all restraints' – as, apparently, was the restored monarch himself, King Charles II. William Wycherly's comedy *The Country Wife* was considered the 'most obscene' – they had degrees of obscenity? Actresses (including Nell Gwynn) appeared for the first time, and we had the first female playwright, Aphra Behn.

Two new Playhouses opened in Drury Lane and Dorset Gardens: both designed by architect Christopher Wren, and fitted with moveable scenery and elaborate machines for thunder, lightning and waves.

In the Victorian theatre the actor-manager moulded plays to suit the capacity of his stage, the taste of his public, the competence of his company – and his own ego. Pictorial stage scenery developed still further during this period when productions retreated behind both a proscenium arch and a huge orchestra pit – a lay-out designed to allow performers in the new 'Italian operas' to see their conductor. Orchestras would fill the pit, even for straight plays which at that time were often written in five acts with musical overtures and intervals. Ashley Dukes described how, at this time, 'a stage manager settled the practical details of production and left the play to take care of itself'.

Perhaps the best-known of these *practical men* was Bram Stoker, general manager to Henry Irving at the Lyceum Theatre, and the author of *Dracula*.

Here are a handful of the 7000 words written by Clement Scott reviewing Irving's production of *Romeo and Juliet*:
'The curtains opened to reveal the market place at Verona. Donkeys, children, a picturesque conduit, a sloping bridge in the background – and the warring Montagues and Capulets turning this fair scene into disorder and fear.

(*later*) Mercutio and Romeo walked through an avenue of torches into Capulet's house, and suddenly the curtain lifted on the banquet. Serving men removed peacocks from the table, Rosaline was seated on a throne of blue and silver flanked by silver draperies and surrounded by scarlet oleanders, while in the foreground moved richly-clad pages and serving wenches. The minuet began and crowds of youths and girls moved slowly and rhythmically, displaying their rich Renaissance brocades and satins. The music had been specially composed by Sir Julius Benedict, and unseen singers added voices to the dance melodies. The balcony scene was as richly apparelled as the dancers. Juliet stood on the marble terrace of an ancient palace, beneath a roof supported on huge pillars. Her garden below was filled with real trees, the moon shone on a little rivulet, and around the water grew real lilies, tall and white in the moonlight.

(*later*) Mercutio's death took place outside the city walls of Verona in the glaring heat of the sun, darkened by long lines of cypress trees, and with the red-tiled roofs of buildings stretching away into the distance. The monastery scene was resonant with chanting monks, and the ringing of monastery bells punctuated the action. The most elaborate scene of all was Juliet's bed-chamber; golden lattices, foliage in the garden, the blue sky with rosy fingers of dawn breaking across it'.

Other reviews were briefer: "Dear me: Mr Irving is 43 and Ellen Terry is 30; they are old enough to know better", and "C'est magnifique mais ce n'est pas l'amour". Despite the critics the public flocked to the play: a hundred and sixty-one performances, bringing in £34,000, with a profit of £10,000.

I take particular interest in Clement Scott's description of what appear to be lighting effects: 'the moon shone on a little rivulet'; 'the glaring white heat of the sun' and 'the blue sky with rosy fingers of dawn breaking'. We know that the Lyceum had arc-lights: they highlighted the principals to help them stand out from the crowds: otherwise Irving was dependent on gas. Of a later adaptation of *The Bride of Lammermoor* W Graham Robertson wrote 'the final tableau reveals the incoming tide rippling over the Kelpie's Flow under a sky full of the glory of the dawn – this illusion created simply by Irving's genius with gas lighting'.

'Irving had always been a believer in processions, and his first entrance in *Hamlet* was at the end of a procession *dramatized by music*' according to biographer Madeleine Bingham. 'The solitary figure of Hamlet looked extra-ordinarily tall and thin. He was weary, his cloak trailed on the ground, the hair looked blue-black like the plumage of a crow, the eyes burning, two fires veiled as yet by melancholy'. His leading lady at the Lyceum, Ellen Terry, put it rather more succinctly; 'He was never an ensemble player'. Irving had forged himself into an actor who gave the stage an intellectual flavour, and had a newly (and expensively) refurbished Lyceum Theatre where, he told Stoker, 'I shall be sole master'. He would also be the British theatre's first knight.

Director Peter Brook, in the first of the four lectures published in his book *The Empty Space*, said 'I can take any empty space and call it a bare stage. A man walks across this empty space whilst someone else is watching him, and this is all that is needed for an act of theatre to be engaged'.

I have summarised the way that the *empty space* of the Greek theatre became the enclosed, cluttered space of Irving's Lyceum Theatre, stage separated from the audience by a proscenium arch, an orchestra pit and footlights. There have been many and varied attempts over the years to restore the stage-audience relationship, the most recent (at the time of writing) being Sir Nicholas Hytner's Bridge Theatre, just across the river from the site of Burbage's Playhouse.

It was another Blackfriars theatre, Sir Bernard Miles's Mermaid (*above*), which first made me aware of the wonderful atmosphere occasioned when both audience and performers share the same space. The raked auditorium and the foot-high stage were fitted inside the four stone walls of an old warehouse. No barriers: no orchestra pit, no footlights, no front curtain. Indeed, often no back curtain or cyclorama: sometimes just the stone wall.

We were all in it together, and shared in the fun as Hy Hazel sang *When does the ravishing begin?* in the Mermaid's 1959 production of *Lock up Your Daughters*.

Joan Littlewood said 'I have built my life on the rock of change'. Audiences often saw the rear walls of the stage in her Theatre Royal at Stratford East where I learnt so much, and developed some of my closest theatre friendships, but that episode in my career can wait for a later chapter.

I'll end this chapter with a relevant memory of Bristol's Theatre Royal, home of the Bristol Old Vic. The Regency-style auditorium has tiers of seats in the form of a horseshoe. There was a proscenium; there was an orchestra pit: the overall dimensions, however, somehow suggested that the horseshoe curve was repeated around the rear of the stage, hinting at a complete amphitheatre encompassing both stage and audience in the one space. Certainly the atmosphere inside the auditorium, and the *blazing performances* on the stage worked their magic and, like Tom Stoppard, I was *turned onto theatre*.

CHAPTER TWO
ON THE OUTSIDE, LOOKING IN

For much of my career I have been watching performances from the lighting control box or from the stage manager's desk in the prompt corner. On the outside, looking in. A familiar position. My most popular Talk is titled *The View from the Wings*.

Walking to school every morning I would pass the front doors of Bromley's New Theatre (now the old theatre, having been replaced in 1977 by the Churchill). I never saw the inside, although the regularly-changing posters each side of the doors made me familiar with the titles of plays, and the names of the playwrights. Whether because of tight finances or lack of parental enthusiasm for live entertainment we were never taken to a play – although I do remember a Christmas production of *Where the Rainbow Ends* with Anton Dolan as St George, probably at Streatham Hill Theatre. I did once talk mother into taking me to the Lewisham Hippodrome, to a variety show starring the ventriloquist Peter Brough who, with his dummy Archie Andrews, was known to us through his weekly broadcasts on BBC radio. Yes, really: a ventriloquist's dummy starred in a radio show!

On that same Hippodrome bill was Ossie Noble; a shy mime artist, who was supposed to be cleaning a statue of a naked lady with a feather duster but was clearly nervous about dusting the naughty bits. A brilliant performance: a man entertaining an audience and making a living with just a statue and a feather duster. Many years later I remembered Ossie Noble when I watched another happy man with a tambourine and a cloth cap. Maybe you see a theme developing here? Incidentally, Ossie had a second career as drummer with a band called the Rolling Stones. No, not *The* Rolling Stones.

I don't recall ever having seen (or read) a play at this time: my knowledge of drama must have come via BBC radio; probably from Saturday Night Theatre and/or the Afternoon Plays. I probably imagined that a live play would be a similarly pleasing-but-uninvolving experience until my first pantomime, at Penge Empire, when I discovered that a live audience could indeed get involved – and that performers in a scripted production could actually talk directly to the audience.

That experience led to my participation in the House Play competition at school and, in my fifth year, a small part in the annual school play. Sadly, but perhaps as an early preparation for my theatrical life to come, financial restrictions forced the production of a thriller instead of the usual Shakespeare or Shaw, so instead of wearing tights I was in a policeman's

uniform (even at fifteen I was already six feet tall with size ten feet). The play was *I Killed the Count* by Alec Coppel (later filmed by Alfred Hitchcock). A thriller, but I got my first laugh – an experience you never forget.

My first experience of Shakespeare was Olivier's film version of *Henry V*. The entire school went to a special morning screening at a Beckenham cinema. I couldn't have wished for a better introduction.

Radio was as close to *culture* as we got in our Bromley home. There were no books, there was no record player. This may have influenced the headmaster's decision to put me into a science stream, well away from any contact with English literature; a decision made without any consultation with, or input from, me. Is one educated to widen one's knowledge, to develop existing talents or interests, or as seems to have happened in my case, to meet some distant Whitehall office's perceived demand for more scientists? Whichever, his decision proved my single biggest handicap when I did eventually get involved in professional theatre.

I'm reminded of a drawing, Victorian in style although possibly not in production, of two children hand-in-hand in the snow (Christmas, perhaps), looking through a window watching a happy family party taking place inside. Standing outside, looking in. There's something interesting going on, but it didn't involve them. I know that feeling, and I also know that I'm not alone. Outsiders come in many professions, many nationalities, and for many reasons: TS Elliot, the American poet, for instance, wrote about being an outsider in England *where one feels always the foreigner: always coming up against differences of feeling that make one feel humiliated and lonely*. I have often felt an Outsider, and we shall meet others during my search.

Even if my parents could have afforded it (which they couldn't), and given my increasing interest in the Arts, I didn't see any point in staying on for a sixth form of Physics, Maths and Applied Maths. My O-level results were good enough to get me into the Borough Treasurer's Department at Fulham, where the Council Offices had a reasonably-well-equipped hall. By volunteering for box office or FOH duties I not only saw the occasional show but also got paid overtime, and it was there that I saw my first amateur Gilbert & Sullivan production. The Town Hall also provided my introduction to 'bureaucracy' and to 'committees' – an essential part of any arts training in Britain.

An amateur drama group in Westminster advertised for men for a production of *I Am a Camera*, a 1951 Broadway play by John Van Druten adapted from Christopher Isherwood's novel *Goodbye to Berlin*. With National Service looming I couldn't make any long-term commitments, but agreed to help out back-stage – until I was thrown on at the dress rehearsal to cover for the American visitor, Clive Mortimer, and played the part for the rest of the week.

National Service took me to Bristol, where Mick and I discovered Peter O'Toole and the Old Vic, and got involved in a couple of productions with an amateur group, the Tudor Players – helping backstage for the first, and appearing in the second, another thriller. Janet Green's *Murder Mistaken*. Mick played Edward Bear, a gentleman who had the nasty habit of killing off his wives for their money and I, inevitably, was the policeman who eventually arrested him.

At the end of studies in Bristol we flew out to Hong Kong. Our work schedules there ruled out any theatrical involvement – although the new cinema which opened on our Small Wave Bay base on the island provided an occasional touch of 'culture', and reclaimed land below the base provided an excellent sports field. I even got into the hockey team – they were that desperate for players. A year in Hong Kong sounds glamorous, but our National Service pay didn't permit too much involvement in the Colony's attractions, so, once again, I often found myself on the outside, looking in.

CHAPTER THREE
THE STORY SO FAR . . . .

'Old men ought to be explorers' wrote T S Eliot. Well, I'm certainly an old man (now 81), and celebrating – if that's the word – the sixtieth anniversary of my first theatre appointment. Many of my early posts were backstage or in the front office, remote from the planning/production/ rehearsal processes, and therefore in ignorance of the theories developed or followed during those processes. Minimalism, for instance, or Realism, Brechtian Alienation, English Puritan Romantic! When, later, I started to write and direct, I simply 'told a story' – writing and staging my stories in whatever dramatic (or cinematic) form seemed most suitable.

So, to please T S Eliot, this book is in part an *exploration*; a trip back through a theatrical past to fill in gaps, flesh out memories, comprehend some of the theories. Joining me for parts of the journey will be Mr G Bernard Shaw, responsible (with Peter O'Toole) for my choice of career, and cropping up regularly in my travels not least in the eventual discovery of *my tambourine*.

Shaw excelled at making tragic fun of Henry Irving who, although specializing in Shakespeare, *understood not a word of his plays*. In the Saturday Review he dramatised the ghastly struggle between Irving and Shakespeare, urging his readers to bear in mind the venerable actor's deep sincerity in preferring his own treasons *to the unmutilated masterpieces of the genius on whom he had lavished lip-honour. My regard for Sir Henry Irving*, he continued, *cannot blind me to the fact that it would have been better for us twenty years ago to have tied him in a sack with every existing copy of the works of Shakespeare, and dropped him into the crater of the nearest volcano*. By such tricks did Shaw hope that Irving's entrances on stage would be greeted with uncontrollable bursts of laughter – a fitting penalty for the actor who had become *the despair of all authors and true Shakespeareans*: Shaw naturally included himself in both categories.

 Someone else who attacked the Irving style of presentation – with actions as well as words – was William Poel, the man credited with that renaissance in theatre production styles which became known as the Elizabethan Revival. Poel's diary records *the unforgettable turning point* in his life:

Sunday 11 April 1875: 'Salvini's performance as Othello had astonished me with its primitive ferocity but, for me, his *Hamlet* had an even greater charm. This was a prince in manner as well as birth; and the fact of the part having been studied, not from the familiar acting edition but from the original text, rendered the interpretation free from the inconsistences that displease the Shakespearian student. His Hamlet did not, in the scene with Ophelia, fitfully rush on and off the stage, nor show an undignified irritability in his remarks to Polonius, nor sprawl on the ground in the presence of ladies, nor whine in monotones at each appearance of the Ghost. He was content with natural gestures, a variety of delicate intonations, and very graceful and expressive movements. The dismissal of Ophelia was given with exquisite feeling'.

As Bernard Shaw was to do just six weeks later when leaving Dublin for London to become *a professional man of genius*, Poel gave up a safe office job, in his case with the London architects Lucas, in February 1876. He travelled to Bristol to join the acting company of Charles Mathews - changing his name in the process when the programmes incorrectly printed his family name of Pole as Poel.

He set out to discover all he could about the science of acting and, above all, to study Shakespeare. Over two-and-a-half years, at a guinea a week if he was lucky, he toured the provinces with Charles Mathews and with Osmund Tearle, and had residencies in Dublin and Liverpool.

Back in London he saw Mrs Kendal and Squire Bancroft in *Peril*, and Irving as Richard III: 'There is less exaggeration, and Irving's comedy touches are good, but the last scenes exhibit all his old weaknesses. He appears to aim at creating an effect by working his scene up to a striking picture upon which the curtain may fall. This is a modern practice that I much dislike as it is sensational and stagey'.

After a summer season in Oxford with Clifford Cooper, Poel joined James Scott's company to tour tiny venues in the North  Riding of Yorkshire, often walking from town to town alongside a donkey cart carrying their few props and possessions. Payment would be 'a share of the takings'; takings often reduced by opposition in the form of a travelling circus or music hall. Once he had to part with a pair of trousers to pay the landlady: on another occasion he sold his watch to pay their rail fares to Malton. Returning home in June 1878, Poel saw Irving in *Vanderdecken*, and found him *even more mannered and faulty*. 'I wouldn't give Irving five pounds a week' said Poel before admitting 'He is wonderful in a way, but it is not my way'.

Robert Speaight's wonderfully-researched and detailed biography picks up the story: 'In the winter of 1878 Poel went on tour in the provinces giving solo recitals from Shakespeare, Sheridan, and other classical playwrights, picking up an audience wherever he could. 'Shakespeare was a practical man of the theatre', he insisted; 'we had to follow his intentions to make it manifest'.

Poel believed that this involved 'rapid, highly-coloured, musical speech of great range and flexibility, creating magic with the mere sound of words', and reforming the over-emphatic declamatory style of speaking forced on actors performing in larger theatres such as the Lyceum.

He established the Elizabethan Stage Society in 1894, the year of his marriage to Ella Locock. The Society's first *recitals* were *Richard II* and *Romeo and Juliet*. He often cast women in male roles, and his Romeo was played by Lillah McCarthy: she wrote about her first meeting with Poel, 'a gracious smile on his handsome gentle face - and giving life to Shakespeare's dramas, doing so easily what others had so often found impossible; reconciling the poetic and the dramatic in his plays by showing they are not contradictory but complementary to one another'.

Bernard Shaw saw Miss Lillah McCarthy play Lady Macbeth in Poel's production for the Shakespeare Reading Society in the St George's Hall: 'She can hold an audience even while she is doing everything wrongly. The banquet scene and the sleepwalking scene were quite successful; and if the earlier scenes were immature, unskilful, and entirely artificial and rhetorical in their conception, they were very nearly thrilling. I should like to see Miss McCarthy play again'. He would, of course, see her often, and eventually in his own plays. Even later his plays would be staged under her management.

The first full production (rather than *recital*) by the Elizabethan Stage Society was *Twelfth Night* given in June 1895 in Burlington Hall, Saville Row, and then St George's Hall. Captain Hutton, who had been *shocked* by the defective swordsmanship on the London stage, was on hand to offer technical advice, and Arnold Dolmetsch superintended the music. *Twelfth Night* was played with a single interval of just ten minutes. Ben Greet was present, and immediately engaged Lillah McCarthy (a red-wigged Olivia) to play leading parts in a tour of Shakespeare's plays.

In July 1896 Poel turned St George's Hall into a facsimile of the Elizabethan Fortune Theatre for his first non-Shakespearian production, *Dr Faustus*, by Christopher Marlowe, reprised in October at the Royal Court Theatre.

Shaw was there: 'The more I see of these performances by the Elizabethan Stage Society, the more I am convinced that their method of presenting is not only right for that particular sort of play, but that any play performed on a platform amidst the audience gets closer home to its hearers than when it is presented as a picture framed by a proscenium'.

However, this sustained activity and, in particular, the quality of the costuming, had cost money, most of it from Poel's private purse. Shaw wrote to him:

30 March 1898:

'I am perfectly paralysed by your balance sheet. I myself have just had to fork out more than £50 to wind up the Independent Theatre solvently (J T Grein's Independent Theatre had produced Shaw's first play *Widower's Houses*), but your £917.16s.7d takes my breath away. I have often wondered at the recklessly handsome way in which the ESS dressed its performances. If I had thought that you were standing the racket yourself, I should certainly have remonstrated with you like a father. All I can do is seize the occasion of your forthcoming performance to do what I can through the Saturday Review to let people know what you have done, and what they must do if you are to continue'.

Shaw kept his word: The Saturday Review, 16 April 1898: 'Mr Poel has achieved artistic originality, beauty, and novelty of effect: nothing like the dressing of his productions has been seen by the present generation. The last few performances show not only that he has succeeded in forming a company of most considerable promise, but that a tradition of Elizabethan playing is beginning to form itself in the Society.

It seems a pity that the Society should succumb just as it is getting into shape, and beginning to understand its business thoroughly'. With Shaw's help, the ESS survived.

In 1910 Beerbohm Tree invited Poel to present *The Two Gentlemen of Verona* in His Majesty's Theatre as part of a Shakespeare Festival. For the first time an apron was built out over the orchestra pit, and front lighting installed in the balconies; an arrangement later repeated by Beerbohm Tree himself for his own production of *Henry VIII* in 1912.

Edith Evans first appearance on stage was with a local amateur group, the Streatham Shakespeare Players, run by an elocution teacher Miss Massey. William Poel saw her there, *the best Beatrice I have ever seen*, and cast her as Cressida opposite Esme Percy's Troilus at the King's Hall. She was then twenty-two years old, without any formal stage training. 'You don't need exams for acting; you need courage', she said. Poel himself played Pandarus, and a young Hermione Gingold was Cassandra.

Sir Peter Hall, first Director of the Royal Shakespeare Company (of which more later) called William Poel *the great Shakespearean revolutionary*. The first time Peter Hall worked with Edith Evans he *made her sit down night after night and teach me what Poel had taught her*.

This was, primarily, that 'Shakespeare wrote lines, not words. That the iambic pentameter, which is like the system under-lying a piece of jazz, has a strong rhythm, and needs marking as a line. You keep the beat, you preserve the line, but it's how you nearly break the line which enables you to express both the emotion and the feeling – and that feeling is the actor's choice: Shakespeare doesn't tell the actor what to feel. He does tell you where you pause, where you come in on cue, where you go fast, or go slow. He does tell the actor which words to accent, but leaves it to the actor to work out why'.

'As an opera singer starts with the score, so a Shakespearean actor starts with the text. First, what do I say? Then, how do I say it?' Well, according to Edith Evans, 'you don't breathe in the middle of a line, for instance; you breathe at the end. You try to keep your lungs full so that you can control the whole line, but mostly it's the sense: that is the central tradition'. I remember Dame Edith telling a group of students 'draw the end of the line towards you, like reeling in a fish'. 'People like Gielgud, Evans, Ashcroft, even Olivier, were marinated in Shakespearean verse as young actors', said Hall, 'and did it almost without thinking, almost without knowing'. He was concerned that 'our young actors don't do enough Shakespeare: they can't get their tongues around it, they can't breathe in the right place and end up losing their voices and being quite incomprehensible. It's not a mystique, and it's not hard: it takes approximately a fortnight to learn. Then it's like riding a bicycle'.

Judi Dench claims that she learned about speaking verse at Stratford. 'The rules are that you obey the punctuation and you obey the line ends and don't run on; that half-lines must be half-lines'.

I joined up with the Royal Shakespeare Company as lighting control operator when they took over the Aldwych as their London base in December 1960, opening with John Webster's play *The Duchess of Malfi*. The repertoire included five Shakespeare productions over the first two years – all totally and enjoyably comprehensible; intelligently spoken – with everyone obeying the line ends and the punctuation.

Compared with Irving's productions the plays were simply presented, making full use of the new thrust apron stage which, with a nod in the direction of William Poel and Granville-Barker, had been built out over the orchestra pit.

CHAPTER FOUR: ANNIE HORNIMAN AND THE GAIETY THEATRE, MANCHESTER

Saturday 21st April 1894 saw the first performance of a new play by GBS, *Arms and the Man* at the Avenue Theatre (now the Playhouse) as part of a season financed largely by an anonymous backer. To those in the know, this 'angel' was Annie Horniman; single, 34, *tall, slender, not unattractive, with a sly wit.*

Jonathan Croall described her as *a striking figure, smoking Turkish cigarettes in a long holder, and dressing unconventionally in rich brocades in startling colours.*

Her grandfather had died the previous year, leaving over £300,000, of which £40,000 was Annie's share. Her greatest interests were travel and the arts: in 1899 she had seen Ibsen's *The Enemy of the People* in Munich, and she returned to the Residenz Theater in 1891 for *Hedda Gabler* - with the playwright himself in the audience.

The censor, the Lord Chamberlain – a member of the Royal Household, not a member of the government – had given judgement that *all the characters in Ibsen's plays appear to be morally deranged.*

This same Lord Chamberlain had also banned the second and third plays penned by Bernard Shaw; *The Philanderer* and *Mrs Warren's Profession* (his first had been *Widower's Houses*, given just two performances by J T Stein's Independent Theatre in 1890). Shaw responded to the bans by writing directly to the censor. 'Sir. I am not an ordinary playwright in general practice. No! I am a specialist in immoral and heretical plays. I write such plays with the deliberate object of transforming public opinion to mine in these matters. If you prevent me from staging such plays' he added, 'I shall propagate my views through the publication of books, over which you, the censor, have no control'.

Which is what he did; publishing his three *Plays Unpleasant*, each with added lengthy prefaces, legally offering to the reading public those self-same scripts which could not be legally performed in a public theatre. However, the bans had seriously affected his income: he desperately needed a profitable play; a comedy, perhaps? Something innocuous to satisfy the censor? The result, the wonderful result was the simple, small-cast, very funny, three-act comedy *Arms and the Man* which, thanks to Miss Horniman's anonymous financial backing, was about to get its first performance. The producer was Shaw's current lady friend, Florence Farr, who was also playing the role of Louka.

Miss Florence Farr.

Annie and Florence were friends, and fellow members of a secret occult society, the Order of the Golden Dawn. Annie's support for the new iconoclastic drama was also secret: her parents would certainly not have approved. Critic William Archer described *Arms and the Man* as 'one of the most amazing entertainments at present before the public. It is quite as funny as *Charley's Aunt*: we laughed wildly, hysterically'. However the seats were not filled, and Annie lost around £4000. She was then in London, working as an unpaid secretary to W B Yeats around the time he was forming the Irish Literary Society.

The Society booked the Antient Concert Rooms in Dublin and, with a company recruited and rehearsed in London (by Florence Farr), they performed for a week with *The Countess Cathleen* by Yeats, and *The Heather Field* by Edward Martyn. Max Beerbohm followed them across and wrote 'Despite the little cramped stage and the tawdry scenery, I was conscious that a beautiful play was being enacted, and I felt that I had not made the journey in vain'. Similar seasons in the following two years led to the formation of the Irish National Theatre: Annie helped them with costumes and scenery - and finance – making the Abbey Theatre the first endowed theatre in Britain (1904). Annie was not there: as a result of constant rows with Yeats during rehearsals she had returned to London to concentrate on management which could be done from there, and giving up on costume making and design.

Eventually, Annie had enough of Yeats and the Irish temperament, and cut off the finances. She had a better offer: her *Tambourine Moment*? Annie had taken the Irish Players to Manchester, impressing a local critic, James Agate. She, in turn, was impressed by the ballroom of the Midland Hotel; a stage at one end and rows of pretty boxes down each side. With her manager, local man Ben Iden Payne, she informed the newspapers of their plans to form a repertory theatre in Manchester. Payne drew his actors from Granville Barker's company, Frank Benson's company, and William Poel's Elizabethan Stage Society. Their first season included Shaw's first play *Widower's Houses,* 'a great success'.

Ibsen and Shaw had helped to change public attitudes and there was a new climate in which Annie's dreams could grow. Encouraged by this early success she bought the Gaiety Theatre in Peter Street and opened it on Saturday 11th April 1908 with *Measure for Measure*.

Annie's supporters were a motley crowd; actor Basil Dean (playing Claudio for only 35 shillings a week) described them as 'general marchers in the advance guard of public opinion'.

Their first surprise was the bare, Elizabethan-style stage on two levels set within the proscenium arch. Musicians from the Palm Court Orchestra at the Midland Hotel played Elizabethan airs, adding to the atmosphere. William Poel directed, and played Angelo: the Isabella was Sarah Allgood, borrowed from the Abbey Theatre. Also in the company was Esme Percy, described by Basil Dean as *an exotic flower in Miss Horniman's prim herbaceous border*.

Basil Dean recalled that 'all sorts of rumours about Poel's eccentric methods preceded his arrival; and his peculiarities of speech and manner were mercilessly burlesqued in the dressing room by us youngsters. He strode about the stage like some great black bird, with flapping arms protruding from a black cape and hands usually encased in black woollen gloves. His beautiful aquiline features shone with ascetic zeal as he expounded his views on the rendering of the part to each individual player, some of whom resented his close teaching. I soon discovered there was method in Poel's insistence on the incantation of the Shakespearean line, and I spent long hours in solitary instruction with him, repeating the lines until my head was in a whirl. In the end I found Poel had taught me the secret of rhythmic speech, the value of the operative word, and the magic of Shakespeare when it is spoken both musically and intelligently. Those lessons – for that is what they were – I have never forgotten'.

The impact of Poel's ideas upon Miss Horniman's company was 'like a fresh sea breeze in a rather self-satisfied atmosphere, achieving a total effect of surge and sweep quite unlike anything heard before, the exhilaration of which remains still in the memory'.

C E Montague, in the Manchester Guardian: 'Mr Poel worked wonders: the proscenium arch prevented the Elizabethan sensation of having an actor come forward to the edge of the platform to deliver speeches in the midst of ourselves but, better than ever, we saw the needlessness, as well as the destructiveness, of the quite modern method of tackling Shakespeare's shortest scenes which are usually scurried through by actors maintaining a precarious footing on a strip of boarding between the footlights in front and a bellying canvas landscape behind. In Mr Poel's Elizabethan arrangement a roomy front portion of the stage is divisible from the rest by a curtain which can either be passed through at its middle or walked round at its ends; the rear portion of the stage is in turn divisible into two or more planes of distance as it retreats into the 'tiring house' at the back. With this arrangement short scenes and long ones flow into one another without the slightest jolt or scrappiness. The use of the 'upper stage' was also surprisingly effective; it made you see why Shakespeare's stage directions so often bring in people 'above'; 'on the walls', or otherwise aloft. Mr Poel's own acting seizes you up and makes you more intimate with his character'. There were reservations about Poel's Victorian *puritanical* editing of the text, such as 'he will shortly be a father' replacing 'he has got a wench with child'.

The production was a tremendous success at the Stratford Festival (April 1908): 'one of the theatrical sensations of my life' according to the Daily Telegraph critic, and Barry Jackson was bowled over by the directness, simplicity and verve of the production. 'I always knew there was something wrong with productions that needed long intervals to set up elaborate scenes that would only last a few minutes. Irving's twenty minute interval whilst an elaborate garden scene was set for the short fifth act of *The Merchant of Venice*, for instance; and a very popular production of *The Taming of the Shrew* by Oscar Asche and Lily Brayton when I had a sensation that the audience spent as much time looking at the tableau curtain as at the comedy itself.

The impetus of Poel's *Measure for Measure* encouraged Barry Jackson to form his own company, the Birmingham Repertory Theatre, in 1913.

Sybil Thorndike wondered if Annie's pioneer work was fully appreciated by the people of Manchester. Sybil met and married Lewis Casson when they were in the Gaiety company: she 'liked Miss Horniman awfully: she looks as if she'd stepped out of a mid-Victorian picture – tall and dignified and a beautiful face, and she wears the most wonderful clothes'.

In 1909 Annie Horniman arranged a London season for her Gaiety company at the Coronet Theatre: 'not exactly West End, but not too expensive'. Shaw was in the audience for their first night offering, his own play *Widower's Houses*. In the opposite box sat Ellen Terry. E A Baughan wrote in the Daily News: 'Go to the Coronet and see the company turn itself inside out from night to night so that you don't know on which side they shine most'.

By 1910 Miss Horniman had eighty on the payroll: performers, production staff and theatre staff. Sufficient actors for two companies, half to rehearse or tour, the others *playing*, all on forty-week contracts. Wages ranged from £3 to £12. Those who left went with her blessing. Sybil Thorndike and Lewis Casson moved to London, returning in 1911 when Casson took over from Ben Iden Payne as Artistic Director. Glasgow had already formed a Repertory company when, in 1910, Basil Dean and Miss Darragh left to start another in Liverpool where Annie and Granville-Barker encouraged businessmen to endow the new organisation. She loaned them costumes and sets, and when their first production, *Strife*, opened 20 February 1911 the London press were in the audience. The trial season made a profit of £1,600. Annie next cajoled 'the good people of Sheffield'.

Manchester had a sell-out success with Galsworthy's *Justice,* recently seen as the opening production of the Vedrenne/Barker season at the Duke of York's Theatre in London. Lewis Casson's first big production on his return was *Twelfth Night* for the Christmas season of 1911: another great success. However, *Julius Caesar*, directed by Casson was described as 'an unconventional, freakish *Gordon Craigy* production'. Annie was horrified: she abhorred any artistic inspiration that owed allegiance to Gordon Craig who had rudely criticised her at the time of her split with Yeats and the Irish Theatre – mainly for being a woman. Casson tended his resignation, but a public front of sweet reasonableness was assumed with an announcement that Mr Casson would do two further productions before taking up the post of Artistic Director with the Glasgow Repertory Company. In wartime conditions, with no younger men available, Miss Horniman managed an amazingly varied programme of comedy at the Gaiety but eventually the war took its toll, and she was forced to suspend operations at the end of a summer season in Blackpool in 1917. The Gaiety continued as a venue for touring productions (in May 1920 hosting Noel Coward's *I'll Leave It To You* with the twenty-year-old author in the cast) but on 3rd October 1920, Annie – by then aged 60 - was forced to sell the Gaiety to clear a large overdraft. Manchester's loss was London's gain: Annie Horniman's policies were adopted by Lilian Baylis in her successful operation of London's Old Vic Theatre.

Annie Horniman died 6 August 1937. 'She was as generous with her time as with her money' said Yeats (*who drew this sketch*). Lewis Casson compared her to a small Australian tree which the natives called *the good mother* because it has to die before its seeds can germinate and blossom. Shaw said that her work deserves to live as long as the British Theatre.

CHAPTER FIVE
DIRECTORS AND DIRECTING

I was eighteen when I saw Peter O'Toole at Bristol and decided on a future career in the theatre, and almost twenty-one when I got my first theatre job. All I knew about directing at that time was what I had read in books by Edward Gordon Craig. 'The relationship of the director to the actor is precisely the same as that of the conductor to his orchestra. He takes the copy of the play from the dramatist, and promises faithfully to interpret it as indicated in the text. During his first reading of the play the entire colour, tone, movement and rhythm that the work must assume comes clearly before him'. Hmm!

The director Sir Richard Eyre described himself as a *latecomer* to the theatre: he was fifteen when he saw a play called *Hamlet* of which he knew almost nothing (he admitted to being a science nerd). He knew even less of the actor playing the title role – Peter O'Toole in his unreconstructed state, dark-haired, wild, violent, mercurial and thrilling, before stardom and Lawrence of Arabia turned him blonde and small-nosed – but his performance as Hamlet *hooked Richard onto theatre*. It was Peter Hall's later Stratford production of *The Wars of the Roses* – swift, graphic, unsentimental, brilliantly acted, bringing Shakespeare into the world of contemporary power politics - which convinced Richard that he wanted to be a director.

Richard did become one of our most successful directors - at Leicester, Edinburgh and Nottingham before succeeding Peter Hall at the National Theatre where he remained for ten years. We have strangely just missed each other on our theatrical journeys: I was in Edinburgh with Scottish Opera until just before he took over at the Royal Lyceum Theatre: I had departed Nottingham Playhouse by the time he arrived there to replace Stuart Burge, and I was well clear of the National Theatre (then still at the Old Vic) long before he took over the National's South Bank Mausoleum.

 Given this impressive breadth of experience, Richard Eyre's views on 'the role of the Director' might serve to ease us into this chapter.

'Directing is an activity of which audiences are largely unaware unless it is intrusively self-advertising, and which even its practitioners find hard to define and harder still to describe. It's something you do, like gardening and like gardening, you only learn about it by doing it.

Directing is the process of understanding the meaning of a play and staging it in the light of that knowledge, underscored by a view of what the writer is trying to say, and why. With some playwrights (political playwrights such as David Hare, for instance) the *why* is as important as the *what*. In rehearsal the writer provides the actors with the territory to be explored and the director draws the map of the journey. Directors cannot play God: they are negotiators, diplomats, mediators - suspended between the writer's need to impel the play forward and the actor's desire to stand still and create a character.

Directors are the builders, not the architects, and with a new play there will always be a tension – more often than not a fruitful one – between the author and director: an implicit competition for territory that has to be negotiated by both parties with a blend of self-effacement and self-assertion. This accounts for the fact that some directors work exclusively on the classics, where the author is obligingly unable to be present at rehearsals.

Tennessee Williams said 'the playwright has two alternatives. Either he must stage the play himself or he must find a director who has the very unusual combination of actively-creative imagination plus a true longing or even just a true willingness to devote his own gifts to the faithful projection of someone else's vision. This is a thing of rarity.

Stuart Burge was such a 'thing of rarity': he replaced John Neville at Nottingham Playhouse during a period of discontent over John's dismissal, and was the perfect choice in that situation: an excellent director, with good contacts and a superb temperament – unlikely to upset anyone. His contract acknowledged that  he had some ongoing film and TV commitments, and that there would be guest directors (in that first season Jonathan Miller, William Chappell and Michael Blakemore) and that they would be working in repertoire with two or three changes of programme every week. The guest directors would, of course, disappear after their first nights. Someone had to be recruited to the new post of Repertoire Manager to maintain both artistic and technical standards of all productions in the repertoire. That someone was me, and I was fortunate indeed to have that experience of working for and with Stuart Burge.

Richard Eyre was his successor there, and has similar memories: 'Stuart was gifted and lucid as a director. He cast well, he cared about narrative – and cared in the right way about what the audience understood and what they felt. And he loved actors. You underestimated him at your peril: he was very shrewd – canny, really – and sometimes calculating. He could be very tough but he was also tender and generous and quite without envy. We all need luck, especially the luck of having people take an interest in you at the right time in your life'. For Richard, Stuart Burge was 'part of my luck. He approached me when I didn't know what to do with my life, and he became a friend and mentor for thirty years. He never changed: he always had that air of being both amused and bemused by life. He always looked the same – the knotted silk scarf round his neck beneath the boyish face, a pair of half-moon glasses straying distractedly somewhere or other, and a chuckle at some new absurdity that had come his way. What survives for me of Stuart is my memory of a droll, humane and gifted man who was forever young'.

I whole-heartedly second all of that, as well as playwright Peter Barnes' comment in his obituary following Stuart's sadly-early death: 'He looked like a bemused gnome who had turned vagueness into a higher art form'. Certainly Stuart believed that 'every decision made on any production must stem from the text – whether a classic or a new play' and as both writer and director I totally support that. How the story is told is up to the director, but it is the author's story and the author must be respected – although I had some sympathy for John Dexter when he reprimanded Arnold Wesker 'Shut up, Arnold, or I'll direct this play the way you've written it'.

Peter's obituary ended 'Stuart admired actors and respected good scripts, and he did his job, wonderfully transforming craft into art. In a floating world he was the real thing'.

Stuart didn't rush into decisions: there would be an 'er' or three before any answer but I soon learned that during that pause he had considered all the possible alternative answers and invariably selected the right one – probably as a result of his wide experience in films and television where any directorial decision has to consider camera angles, running time, lighting, costume and set changes – and a wrong answer could cost considerable time and money.

Stuart had started as an actor alongside Edith Evans in a pre-war Michel Saint-Denis production of *The Witch of Edmonton*. Irving Wardle reported that he auditioned for George Devine's Young Vic company by reciting *You are old, Father William* while standing on his head.

His Young Vic experiences helped him to formulate a *golden rule*: 'the need to bend a performance to accommodate audience response, and particularly so with younger audiences. It was necessary', he felt, 'to create a tight structure within which the actors should be capable of improvising'. That golden rule has served me extremely well in my *post-tambourine* career as a solo speaker/performer.

Sir Nicholas Hytner was Trevor Nunn's successor at the National Theatre: 'British audiences don't expect a facsimile of the original production, but they won't go with a director beyond the point where they lose sight of the playwright. They want a production which gives them the play they've come to see, which still leaves a  director with a vast amount of room to manoeuvre – but they usually smell a rat if the play is nothing more than a vehicle for the director's imagination. That imagination should reveal the play, rather than the other way around'. This leaves too much room in the British theatre for the kind of production that does no more than apply a coat of gloss to a play and leaves it to fend for itself. Nicholas says that he would far rather see a director go out on a limb than draw an intellectual blank. 'You can count on an audience knowing enough about *Hedda Gabler* to take in an argumentative production, he thought, but if you're inviting them to a play they're unlikely to have seen before, they will want more access to the play than to its director'.

I agree. I have no problem with contemporary productions of the classics, even with their occasional bizarre (and sometimes distracting) switches of period and/or gender: I've occasionally been known to update my own productions – in both drama and opera. It can freshen up a well-known script or, as has happened all-too-often, help to accommodate an impossibly tight budget. At the same time I have some concern for those seeing a classic play – or opera - for the first time, not knowing the plot or the period it was set in, and being confused by the clever directorial touches. If we don't occasionally have access to the real thing, we may not be able to appreciate just how 'clever' those 'directorial touches' are.

Director Franco Zeffirelli had similar thoughts: 'I have, throughout my career, been giving the world's major opera houses new productions of the great classics which will act as their standard repertoire for years to come.

Of course, we have to have *avant-garde* interpretations; of course we can have modern-dress versions of eighteenth-century operas and all the other fun and games, but recently (he was writing in 1980) it did look as if that was all we would have. Surely, every generation must also see the great productions as their creators truly wanted them done, not as pickled museum pieces, but as honest, living interpretations of the author's wishes'.

CHAPTER SIX
LEARNING THE ROPES.

We should perhaps take a chapter out to explain my leap from front office to backstage; from trainee manager with Moss Empires to lighting control operator with the Royal Shakespeare Company at the Aldwych Theatre.

I first entered the Victoria Palace on a Monday morning in late January 1959, still not quite 21, to discover I was going to be working alongside what I considered to be a group of really rather elderly people. Sixty years ago – but I still remember all of their names: Bud Flanagan, Jimmy Nervo, Teddy Knox, Charlie Naughton, Jimmy Gold and Monsewer Eddie Gray. Yes, the wonderful Crazy Gang. My first day in my new career was the first day of rehearsals for what turned out to be their penultimate production, *Clown Jewels*. Highlight of the first half had the entire company all singing *Strolling*, written by Ralph Reader for the Scout's Gang Show, and then bought by the Crazy Gang.

Highlight of the second half had these six elderly misshapen gentlemen dressed as *Disappointed Debutantes* who, due to a change in the rules, were not going to be presented to Her Majesty at the annual Queen Charlotte's Ball. They were in full drag – long dresses, wigs, high heels, handbags, the lot - looking the part - and all joining in the chorus:

> *We've not been presented,*
> *New rules they've invented,*
> *And though we're plumed and scented,*
> *They've not presented us.*

Then they each had a verse: the only one I remember is Charlie Naughton's. He was the shortest, baldest, fattest of the six – still looked stunning in a frock:

> *My three feathers, with much flair,*
> *I stuck firmly in my hair.*
> *They won't let me make my bow.*
> *Where shall I stick my feathers now?*

Their shows were not for the prudish, but they were fun, and sufficiently flexible to accommodate the unexpected. One night Bud Flanagan announced that Sophie Tucker was in the audience, and tried to coax her up on stage. She feigned reluctance, but I could see her musical director Ted Shapiro edging his way along the orchestra pit and, sure enough, as soon as he reached the conductor's rostrum up she went and gave us a heart-rending (and apparently impromptu) rendition of *Some of These Days*.

After a short period at the Victoria Palace I was sent up the road to continue my training at the Palladium, where the pantomime was still running – and would do so until Easter, twice daily, all sold out. That winter (1958/59) the panto was *Sleeping Beauty,* with a cast led by Bruce Forsyth, Charlie Drake, Bernard Bresslaw, Edmund Hockridge and Thelma Ruby. The Palladium was owned by television company ATV so it's no coincidence that three of our 'stars' also had hit TV series at that time. 'Brucie' was actually in the theatre seven days a week since he had just taken over from Tommy Trinder as host of *Sunday Night at the London Palladium*.

Panto was followed by a Spring Show, Frankie Vaughan headlining a bill including Roy Castle, the King Brothers and the Kaye Sisters. Frankie's 'special guest' was the amazing Hetty King, at seventy-five years of age still capable of projecting to the back of the upper circle without a microphone. Then came the Summer Show *Swinging Down the Lane,* with Max Bygraves. Closing the first half, were three hugely energetic American singers, The Peter Sisters.

Manager of the Palladium at this time was Mr George Margrave; distinguished, well-respected, top manager on the Moss circuit – and earning £27 a week, raised to £33 when he came in for the Sunday television transmission. One month into the run of *Swinging Down the Lane* Mr Margrave suggested that as I was approaching the end of my 'training period' I should think about getting measured for a dinner suit. Decision time, although I had already decided. I explained about those visits to the Bristol Old Vic, and my desires to be involved in the practical side of theatrical production. He listened, understood, and – gentleman that he was - arranged for me to join the technical staff back-stage for the next pantomime season.

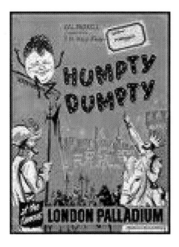

So my next entrance at the Palladium was via the stage door, as props assistant for *Humpty Dumpty* starring the wonderful, irrepressible Harry Secombe, genuinely one of the nicest men you could hope to meet. Harry did hundreds of charity performances: we were chatting in the wings one evening and he showed me a letter he had just picked up at the stage door.

He had agreed to do a midnight matinee charity show, and the letter was to tell him that they had 'done him the honour' of making him top of the bill.

'Some honour' he said. 'Top of the bill at a midnight matinee. All that means is that I sit around in the dressing room smoking and drinking and chatting until about three in the morning. When I do eventually get on I find the entire audience yawning and looking at their watches'. But he did it. He would tell the story of his little grandson watching him put on his dinner suit for yet another charity event and asking him 'Why do you wear that suit, grandpa? You know you always have a headache in the morning'.

Working backstage on a long-running West End pantomime under the guidance of one of the country's greatest stage managers, Jack Matthews, set me up for the next challenge – stage manager in one of the theatres at Butlins Pwllheli Holiday Camp in North Wales for the summer season. Tremendous training for a relative newcomer: you'll remember those entertainers such as Roy Hudd, Cliff Richard, Des O'Connor and Jimmy Tarbuck, who all started their careers as Butlins Redcoats and went on to stardom. Ringo Starr's earliest public performances were in the band in a Butlins Cabaret bar, and the technicians and stage managers similarly gained huge experience during a long and busy summer season. Each camp had two or three theatres; each theatre did at least two shows a day, all with different technical requirements. Everything from major Cabaret Stars on Sundays through professional revues and semi-professional Redcoat shows to camper-participation events. You learnt a great deal – and quickly.

Anyone who visited back-stage in a Butlins theatre around that time will remember that the same notice was stuck on every mirror in every dressing room in every theatre on every camp throughout the country. *Parents don't like it; children don't understand it, and we won't have it at any price* – and you all know what they meant: blue material; bad language. I suspect those signs are long-gone, but in my time they were taken seriously. They even had a monitor speaker up in the management offices so they could check on what was happening on any stage at any time.

One day we had a senior citizen's Talent Contest. One elderly gentleman who fancied his chances as a comic started with a joke about haemorrhoids. To be fair to the old man it was quite funny, but it was also totally tasteless and the management were immediately on their feet, down the stairs, round the back of the theatre, in at the stage door and panting up to my stage manager's desk in the prompt corner yelling 'Get him off'. Sadly, they were much too late: by then he was already well into his second joke which went like this: 'I was walking down the street this morning when I saw my neighbour Bill mowing the lawn without any trousers on. I said to him, Bill, why are you mowing the lawn without any trousers on? and Bill said Well, it's actually the wife's idea: I was trimming the hedge yesterday without my shirt on and I got a stiff neck'. At that point the lights went out, the sound was switched off, the curtains closed and one elderly would-be comic's showbiz career came to an ignominious end.

At the end of each Butlin season I would return to London and check-in with the technicians Union: they also operated as an agency and would know where the current vacancies were. In this way I found myself appointed stage electrician and lighting controller at the Comedy Theatre just at the time they were installing one of the earliest console lighting controls, where one man could sit at a desk (based on an Compton organ keyboard) and control up to 120 circuits single-handed – or even single-footed: there were foot controls as well. These desks have got even more complicated since, but that was one of the first. I was trained to operate it by the men who had designed and installed the system.

Playing at the Comedy Theatre was *A Passage to India*, a transfer from Oxford Playhouse directed by Frank Hauser. A fairly straightforward lighting plot so I soon mastered the intricacies of the new control desk. As with the majority of West End theatres we operated with a very basic crew of full-time technicians, known as *daymen*, with part-timers (*showmen*) joining us for the performances to provide the 'muscle' for scene changes, etc.

Most of the *showmen* had other jobs and were not always available for mid-week matinees so some of us 'moonlighted' to cover matinees at other West End theatres. In this way I was backstage at the Palace on Tuesday afternoons helping with *Flower Drum Song*, and on Thursday afternoons at the Lyric Theatre with an early Peter Brook production, *Irma La Douce*, which I would later stage professionally up in Scotland. I love the show, but it will never be revived by the amateur operatic companies because it has only one female role, Irma herself.

A few months later the Royal Shakespeare Company took over the Aldwych Theatre as their London base, and installed a similar lighting control desk. As the only available operator in London with suitable experience I was recruited by the RSC and, still a relative newcomer to the profession, found myself working alongside people like Dame Peggy Ashcroft (*right*) in the title role of *The Duchess of Malfi*, the opening RSC production at the Aldwych.

CHAPTER SEVEN
HARLEY GRANVILLE-BARKER (1877-1946)

Around the age of twenty-nine or thirty the artist, playwright and stage designer W Graham Robertson once waited upon a Publisher with a picture book. The publisher put it plainly – the pictures and the book were not wanted.
'However, if you would write your reminiscences for us?'
'But I'm not a distinguished person'.
'No, but you have known a great many distinguished people'.
The years passed; most of his distinguished friends had removed to Heaven or to bath-chairs in Bournemouth, and Robertson reconsidered the situation:
'Although I am now old, and still undistinguished, the idea of writing down my memories rather smiles on me. It might be pleasant to wander down the Lanes of Yesteryear'.

His book, *Time Was*, is a fascinating personal reminder of some of the leading painters, sculptors and theatre folk of his time; a volume which has encouraged another *old and undistinguished* writer to attempt something similar within this volume. In particular, I wanted to learn more about my immediate predecessors, those who had brought British theatre to the level where I found it on my arrival in London in 1959.

Robertson's strongest memory was of one of the last London productions by Harley Granville-Barker: 'I have only seen one Shakespeare production which held its own against that of Sir Henry Irving, and that was Harley Granville-Barker's *Twelfth Night* at the Savoy Theatre in 1914 – indeed, it distinctly outshone Irving whose own *Twelfth Night* had been one of the few Lyceum failures; it was wrong in key, it was ponderous and dull. Ellen Terry's lovely Viola seemed to have wandered into it by mistake, her cry of 'What should I do in Illyria?' held a plaintiff note of insincerity, whereas Barker's production was poetic, comic, a delight to the eye yet very simple. It was the work of a true artist'.

This same Harley Granville-Barker is one of my own great personal theatrical heroes; possibly the greatest. Sir Richard Eyre agrees, calling him his 'father-figure. A writer whom I admired more than any twentieth-century English writer before the sixties: Chekhov with an English accent'. William Archer also praised Barker's writing: 'The author of *The Voysey Inheritance* and *Waste* stands, in my eyes, second to none of his contemporaries. I consider these plays (along with *The Madras House*) the biggest things our modern movement has produced'. Not merely a first-rate playwright, Granville-Barker was also the first British director in the way that we now use that term. In Tyrone Guthrie's words, 'In any artistic creation there must be one dominant impulse'. Guthrie himself became one – but by then Granville-Barker had set the standard.

C B Purdom, writing to his film-actor son Edmund: 'I admired Harley Granville-Barker (*right*) more than any other man I had met in the theatre; he was a rare combination of actor, producer, dramatist. Above everything, he was a director, by far the greatest of any whose work I have seen. His is a remarkable story, not to be told without pain for what the theatre lost in him'.

Lewis Casson, in his forward to C B Purdom's excellent biography of Barker, wrote 'As one of the dwindling band who served with Granville Barker in those far-off Court days my remembrance of him is one of vital sensitive youth and energy, a lithe athletic figure, warm brown eyes, thick red-brown hair, tidily parted till he pushed his fingers through it, and an air of relaxed concentration ready to spring in a flash to action or laughter. I remember the confidence he inspired in us all by knowing every play thoroughly before he began to rehearse it.

Barker's method of direction was naturalistic to the extent that the details were drawn from observation of life, and the scale of acting was smaller than the traditional declamatory style. Fine polishing went on right up to the last rehearsal, always by notes taken during the run of a scene, not by interrupting the flow. The whole piece was moulded into a musical and rhythmic pattern as definite as a symphony'.

Harley Granville-Barker (the hyphen was added around the time of his second marriage) wrote, acted in, and directed his own plays, and directed many of Shaw's plays, usually taking the lead roles (written by Shaw with Barker in mind). Together with William Archer they dreamed of, and planned for, the establishment of a National Theatre. They even published a prospectus complete with budgets, and got a foundation stone laid on an island site opposite the V&A Museum – a stone moved so often that the late Queen Mother suggested it should be on castors.

At the age of nineteen Barker had played Richard II for William Poel. He had been introduced to performing as a schoolboy, appearing in his mother's poetry recitals. Aged 13, he was one of thirty-two youths and thirty-five ladies attending what was probably Britain's first-ever theatre school, run by Sarah Thorne who managed the 'stock' company at Margate. Edward Gordon Craig, who acted there briefly, remembers Barker as 'a sickly youth'.

He first appeared on the London stage aged fifteen, playing 3rd Young Man in *The Poet and the Puppets* at the Comedy Theatre. He acted with Lewis Waller; with Ben Greet (alongside Lillah McCarthy), and with Mrs Patrick Campbell. He wrote his first play *The Weather Hen* (with Herbert Thomas) when he was eighteen.

1900 was the break-through year for Granville Barker: his performances for the Stage Society included the role of Robert in Gerhardt Hauptmann's play *The Coming of Peace*.

Shaw attended, was impressed – *not only an actor, but a sensitive, quick, and lively mind bursting with undeveloped energies* - and cast him as Eugene in *Candida*. 'He was the success of the piece' Shaw wrote to William Archer, 'it was an astonishing piece of luck to hit on him'. To Barker, Shaw wrote 'my only misgiving with regard to you is whether the stage in its present miserable condition is good enough for you: you are sure to take to authorship or something of the kind. Meanwhile, you give me the quality of work I want; and I hope to get more out of you before you get tired of it'. Barker next played Captain Kearney in Shaw's play *Captain Brassbound's Conversion* but did, as Shaw had predicted, take to authorship. Again he won Shaw's approval: '*The Marrying of Ann Leete* is a really exquisite play'.

In 1903 businessman J H Leigh bought the Court Theatre in Sloane Square and planned to stage a series of Shakespeare representations. The first two were not particularly well-received and Leigh was advised to 'contact Barker', which he did. Granville-Barker directed *Two Gentlemen of Verona*, opening on 8th April 1904, with Barker himself playing Speed and Lewis Casson as Eglamour, the first time they had acted together. Thyrza Norman was Julia. Their performances, and the production were much praised. Lewis Casson wrote of Granville-Barker's direction of *Two Gentlemen of Verona* 'An impression of youthful authority over a cast who were almost all older and more experienced. He showed immense bodily and vocal skill, and brilliant imagination, without showing off – and the actors welcomed his help and discipline, and respected him. A strong dramatic instinct, a keen intelligence and nobility of character'.

Barker had negotiated with Leigh's manager at the Court, John Vedrenne, for six matinees of *Candida* to be played during the final week of *Two Gentlemen*. These, too, were successful – yielding Shaw £31.3s.0d in royalties. Rather than direct the final Shakespeare offering *Timon of Athens*, Barker chose instead Gilbert Murray's adaptation of Euripides' *Hippolytus* at the Lyric Theatre.

C B Purdom felt that his performances as Eugene Marchbanks in *Candida* and The Messenger in *Hippolytus* surpassed anything that followed. Shaw sang his praises and *had no criticism*; Barker, though, did not feel himself 'a natural actor', being conscious of a deficiency of physical power. All he wanted to do was direct plays, and be playwright in his own theatre. In 1904 Barker and Business Manager John Vedrenne set up their own company to present a contemporary repertoire including plays by Ibsen, Maeterlinck and Shaw at the Court Theatre and with immediate success: on the First Night of Shaw's play *Major Barbara* there were said to be 'almost as many carriages and motor cars in Sloane Square as there are in The Mall'. London theatres had survived for years on the *star* system: one or two top names heading a cast of fairly ordinary *stock* players, but as the critic A B Walkley wrote in The Times 'There is no such all-round acting in London as is nowadays to be seen at the Court Theatre. When all are excellent it is needless to single out individual names'. The season also included Shaw's *Man and Superman* with Granville-Barker in the leading role of John Tanner. For a night or two he went down with influenza and couldn't play: a notice to this effect was pinned above the pay-box, and one playgoer asked what it meant. 'It means that Mr Barker will not be playing John Tanner this evening'. 'Who is Barker?' 'The actor who usually plays John Tanner'. 'But I suppose somebody will play it?' 'Yes, it will be played'. 'Then take my half-crown, and don't make such a fuss'. Audiences went to the Court to see the *play*, not the *actor* and had confidence in the all-round ability of the entire cast. It is perhaps worth noting here that John Tanner was the name of Mrs Patrick Campbell's father.

Under Barker and Shaw a new kind of acting and production began to take root and blossom. They took Poel's theoretical outline, and spread their ideals and enthusiasm through the company and the public so that the aims became a living force. Instead of a dominating actor-manager directing from centre-stage, the group of actors on the stage had a lively audience of one giving them clear directions.

A single line in a minor part would get the same quality of care and attention as any of the great speeches. Once this artistic quality was established, its implications for the theatre of the future could be recognised. Thus it was that with Barker the title of 'Director' began to replace 'Producer'. Barker was credited with 'making directing into a system', and inventing the role of professional director whose sole job it was to bring together all the elements of a production.

The Court Theatre seasons ended in 1907 after more than 800 performances. A grand Criterion Restaurant dinner honoured Barker and Vedrenne; both made speeches, as did Lord Lytton, Herbert Beerbohm Tree and G B Shaw. Barker was eulogised for his inspiring vision of what theatre could be like were it to be freed from the shackles of commercialism and allowed to develop as a fully-fledged art form.

Vedrenne and Barker mounted a much-admired season of Shakespeare at the Savoy Theatre 1912/14. The scenery was said to be 'metaphorical but real; minimal but iconographic' at a time when the prevailing style of Shakespearean productions still went as far as live sheep on stage in *As You Like It*.

(*left*) Barker and Lillah McCarthy (who married in 1906), playing John Tanner and Ann Whitefield in *Man and Superman*. The beard was a deliberate copy of Shaw's.

In 1893 Sir Frank Benson, on tour in Cheltenham with his Company, had heard Lillah McCarthy reciting Prince Arthur from *King John* and, realising her talent, suggested that she be sent to London to be trained. Her brother Dan, himself an actor, introduced her to William Poel.

'The discipline of Mr Poel's rehearsals sometimes wore me down but I was making headway and, after days of scolding from Poel and tears from me, it was arranged that I should read Romeo at the Steinway Hall. *The* Romeo, Henry Irving himself, was in the audience: what would he think of such a *rival*? Afterwards he took my hand, bent over it, and in that voice which none who has heard it can forget, began to praise me. I was hot with blushes, and happy as a queen'.

'During a Shakespeare Society performance of *Macbeth* at St George's Hall the producer came backstage with some exciting news: a well-known critic, one who had written a play and had it acted, was in the front row. He was from the Saturday Review. 'He has red hair, a red beard and a white face.'

Brother Dan patted me on the shoulder and told me not to be afraid. 'He won't eat you' he said; 'it's Mr Bernard Shaw and he's a vegetarian'. 'I was determined to show him how Lillah McCarthy could act Shakespeare. Next morning, Frank Harris in *The World* wrote that I 'walked badly, spoke badly, movements all wrong'. I was petrified – and then the *Saturday Review* arrived: Bernard Shaw had written 'born to act ... great natural ability'. I gulped down the praises. 'Quickly ill; quickly well' said brother Dan, quoting *Cleopatra*. 'The emotions of people of artistic temperament are of an intensity which others can neither experience nor imagine'.

Ben Greet saw Lillah playing Olivia (in that golden wig) in William Poel's production of *Twelfth Night* and engaged her for his Comedy Company. 'The worldly wit of Beatrice proved far beyond my powers (my Muse was Tragedy) but I managed to find gaiety and flamboyance for Peg Woffington. I played Juliet with tenderness and passion, and with unrequited love for my Romeo, H B Irving'. (Henry Irving's son, wearing his father's beautiful Romeo costume).

'Wilson Barrett's representative saw me play Juliet in Edinburgh, and in 1896 I was contracted to join the cast of *The Sign of the Cross* to play Berenice when that play went into the Lyric Theatre, Shaftesbury Avenue, with a weekly salary running into two figures. Penury and Shakespeare were left behind in the provinces. At first I saw Wilson Barrett only as a pompous actor, but found him to be a generous and dear being, a great manager, and a yet greater man behind the affectations. It was with his company that I twice toured Australia, New Zealand and Africa. I had learnt my craft: Wilson Barrett thought me ready to run my own company, and was helping to set up the management in 1904 when he was suddenly taken ill and died'.

Shortly before Barrett's death Bernard Shaw had invited Lillah to his flat in Adelphi Terrace. 'He looked at me, gave a broad smile, and said *Why, here's my Ann Whitfield,* and thus began my association with Shaw and his plays: a new life began for me, the life of the Court Theatre, and of Shaw's *new women*. There was one interlude whilst we were waiting to produce *Man and Superman*: Herbert Beerbohm Tree took me to act with him at His Majesty's Theatre: it was like going away into the country, the atmosphere of the two theatres and the methods of the two producers were so different - Tree using the broader brush of the impressionist, casual but full of inventiveness: Shaw, serious, painstaking, concentrated, relentless in pursuit of perfection'.

'Shaw never harassed us with interruptions in the raw early stages, but his pencil was never still and at the end of each rehearsal we would get plenty to ponder over in the shape of brilliant and brief little personal notes. He would wait for a week before he came up on stage to interfere with our work. Then began a revelation of his knowledge of the theatre and of acting. With complete unselfconsciousness he would show us how to draw the full value out of a line. He could assume any role, any physical attitude, and make any inflection of his voice, whether the part was that of an old man or a young man, a budding girl or an ancient lady.

With his amazing hands he would illustrate the mood of the line. We used to watch his hands in wonder. I learned as much from his hands, almost, as from his little notes of correction'.

'However, after everything has been said about his plays and his philosophy, the best remains unsaid, for the best resides not in his plays, nor in his philosophy, but in his personality. I never knew what a vivid personality meant until I knew Shaw. He, of all men, is most alive, not only on grand occasions but all the time. Walk with him through the streets of any town: a photographer approaches, furtively, but Shaw has seen him and immediately he adds a cubit to his stature. Snap: a perfect picture of the man, tall, resolute, picturesque. It is Shaw's sanity, sentimentality, and lack of humbug which are permanently astonishing even to his friends. His greatest quality – the source of his paradox and his comedy – is that he dares to forge the last link in every chain'.

Lillah McCarthy's 1913 schedule demonstrates the life of a leading actress at that time. 'I began a season of repertory at the Savoy Theatre, with *The Doctor's Dilemma* on Monday evening. The next evening we revived *The Death of Tantagile* followed by *The Silver Box*. For the Wednesday matinee we played *The Doctor's Dilemma* again, and in the evening I played *Nan*. On Thursday we played *The Wild Duck* for the matinee, with *The Doctor's Dilemma* in the evening, repeated on Friday. Saturday afternoon we played *The Witch* with *The Doctor's Dilemma* again in the evening. While doing this the company was also rehearsing every day for *A Midsummer Night's Dream*. In addition I had to share the management of two theatres, The Kingsway and The Savoy.

Harley and Lillah divorced in 1918. Lillah married Dr Frederick Keeble, then Director of the Royal Horticultural Society Gardens at Wisley, later Assistant Secretary at the Ministry of Agriculture, and finally an Oxford Professor, Fellow of Magdalen. He became Sir Frederick, and 'made a

Lady of Lillah'. They bought a field at Boars Hill, shipped the framework of an ancient barn from Herefordshire, and created the most wonderful house, *Hamels,* where Lady Keeble continued to 'entertain' without the need to make-up, or to 'answer the call'. She was friends with the Asquiths, with Sir Austen Chamberlain, and with the designers and artists Charles Ricketts and Charles Shannon, who both painted portraits of her.

Another visitor helped in the garden.

Barker married an American writer Helen Huntingdon: it is believed that in both of his alliances, it was the wife who proposed marriage. Unfortunately, Helen Huntingdon disliked both Shaw and the theatre and, almost certainly under her pressure, the Granville-Barkers moved to France. Out of this self-imposed exile came one major work, slowly assembled over many years: *The Prefaces to Shakespeare.* A primer for actors and directors working on the plays of Shakespeare, aimed at re-establishing the relationship between actor and audience.

His message: 'We have the text to guide us, half-a-dozen stage directions, and that is all. I abide by the text and the demands of the text, and beyond that I claim freedom'.

Like Poel, he argued for a fluency of staging unbroken by scene changes. The verse should be spoken quickly: '*be swift, be swift, be not poetical*' he wrote on Cathleen Nesbitt's dressing room mirror when she played Perdita. Swift – but with meaning.

Paradoxically, he had also written 'If a man believes he can do something then his job is to do it, not talk about it. We have so many producers who confine themselves to showing us in expensively-bound books, and in articles in the high-brow monthlies, how badly we do our job, and how much better they could do it if they tried'. With Granville-Barker's exile to Paris British theatre lost the one man who really should have been *doing something* – and not merely writing about it.

Sybil Thorndike: 'Barker liked actors to use their minds and be creative with ideas. He explained things so beautifully, and would give them a wealth of psychological background. His movements and gestures suggested something of the dancer in him. He had wonderful style and a flexible body, and this astonishingly alive face. He had an electric personality; you came away from rehearsals feeling you'd got a new vision'.

Lewis Casson remembered 'He came at a time when the wealthy patron of taste was dying out, and before the State had recognised the value and necessity of subsidy. We few left that loved him and worked with him in those long-lost days still feel a loyalty to him and to what he stood for, and try to carry on his tradition'.

During WW2 Granville-Barker was in America as a visiting professor at Yale University. He returned to Paris in 1946 and died there on 31st August. The 90-year-old Bernard Shaw was shocked by Barker's death, which *made me realise that I had always cherished the hope that our old intimate relationship might somehow revive.*

CHAPTER EIGHT
INTRODUCING:
'UNCLE JACQUES AND HIS NEPHEW MICHEL'

According to Albert Camus 'The history of the French theatre has two periods – before Copeau and after Copeau'.

Jacques Copeau (1879-1949) was one of the greatest of the French theatrical reformers. His aim was to simplify the stage itself, and his doctrine was summed up in the single phrase  *un tréteau nu*, a bare platform. This was fifty-six years before Peter Brook's *empty space* speech. 'The actor comes out on a platform and acts' said Copeau, 'and that is the essence of theatre. In a time of decadence we should return to the essence'.

Jacques Copeau wrote his first play while still at college, aged 18. He started as a journalist and theatre critic: an early review was of a production of Ibsen's play *A Doll's House*. His second play, written in 1911, was an adaptation of *The Brother Karamazov* – his first step in the fight against 'realism'. Coincidentally, Bernard Shaw's first work on arriving in London was as a journalist, reviewing art, then music, and then theatre. Seeing Ibsen's *A Doll's House* also opened Shaw's eyes to dramatic possibilities, and led to the writing of *his* first play *Widower's Houses*. That premiered in December 1892, preceding Copeau's early efforts.

January 1912. Copeau wanted to rid the Paris stage of the rank commercialism and tawdriness represented by the boulevard theatre, and also the *ham acting* that had become entrenched, even at the venerated Comedie-Francaise.

These he considered obstacles to substantive understanding of the text and to the real development of character. He sought a simpler style freed from the ornamentation that obscured even the finest texts. Armed with these ideals, and with the experience garnered from stagings of his adaptation of *The Brothers Karamazov*, he decided to found a theatre company. He rented the old and dilapidated Left Bank venue, the

Athénée-Saint-Germain on the rue du Vieux - Colombier, and named the theatre after the street so that it could be found more easily.

In the spring of 1913, with the help of Charles Dullin, who had played Smerdiakov in *The Brothers Karamazov*, and in whose Montmartre apartment the auditions took place, Copeau began to assemble a company. This would include the actor/designer/stage manager Louis Jouvet, and Dullin himself, an outstanding actor but with a slightly curved spine which prevented him from taking roles which involved *gazing at the heavens*. Suzanne Bing was a mime expert, and choreographer.

In the summer of 1913 Copeau took his troupe to *Le Limon*, his rural home in the Marne valley and set out his principles for *Le Théâtre du Vieux-Colombier*: First, the choice of venue - far from the despised Right Bank boulevards in a district closer to schools and the centre of artistic life where the new theatre might attract an audience of students, intellectuals and artists with a subscription system that would assure reasonable prices.

Second, a variety of productions - as many as three different productions a week, which would not only appeal to a wider public, but would offer the actors the opportunity to play several different sorts of roles in quick succession, maintaining the suppleness of their interpretive skills.

Third, a repertoire that would include the classics (Racine and Moliere) and the best plays of the past thirty years. Copeau wanted to entice new playwrights, perhaps those who had despaired that the theatre would ever again present works of quality. He also proposed, eventually, a school.

To obtain his *naked stage* Copeau removed from the Vieux-Colombier all of the lyres, garlands, cherubs, mirrors, gilt and chandeliers, all the *gingerbread* that nineteenth century theatres had 'in common with nineteenth century brothels'. The *cadre d'avant-scene* (the proscenium arch) disappeared, as did 75 seats, leaving a stage now half-as-large again as it had been.

The Théâtre du Vieux-Colombier was inaugurated with a little ceremony on 22 October 1913 and opened the next evening with Thomas Heywood's *A Woman Killed By Kindness (Une femme tuée par la douceur)*. Not well received.

Molière's *Amour Médecin*, however, got a more promising reception. Alfred de Musset's *Barberine*, a delightfully poetic piece, charmed the public and showed off the talents of the young company on a bare stage. Dullin triumphed as Harpagon in Moliere's *L'Avare* (*The Miser*) and the troupe showed its physical dexterity in Molière's farce, *La Jalousie du Barbouillé*. A popular revival of the Copeau-Croué adaptation of *The Brothers Karamazov* saw Dullin again as Smerdiakov, Jouvet as Feodor, and Copeau as Ivan.

In May 1914, the troupe, exhausted but buoyed by its artistic and, sometimes critical, successes staged Shakespeare's *Twelfth Night* or *Nuit de Rois*. Both in its preparation and *mise-en-scène*, *Nuit de Rois* has entered into legend.

There were reports of Copeau and Jouvet (who were also performing in the production) working forty-eight hours non-stop to set the lighting and of Duncan Grant, the English artist who created the costumes, chasing after actors to apply one last dab of colour just before curtain up.

The play garnered both critical and public acclaim. In a startlingly simple stage setting, (*right*) with Jouvet as Sir Andrew Aguecheek, Suzanne Bing as Viola, Blanche Albane as Olivia, and Romain Bouquet as Sir Toby Belch, the play called upon the audience's imagination in a way that had not been seen on a Paris stage since Paul Fort in the 1890s. Enthusiastic crowds queued to see 'real Shakespeare', but the run was ended by the outbreak of war.

Copeau was invalided out of the army in 1915. In 1917, probably with some influential help from Clemenceau, he was able to re-establish his Compagnie in New York until their return to France after the war. Copeau's lectures in New York are thought to have influenced the development of post-war American theatre. In France, the impact of the Vieux-Colombier Theatre was also profound.

Copeau's productions of classic plays and the work of new writers promoted a simple, expressive and natural new style. Many years before George Devine voiced similar thoughts, Copeau already 'had in mind the mechanics, property men, and electricians: we must school them as well; a real rapport must establish itself between them and us'.

He also revealed to Jouvet the extent of his debt to Edward Gordon Craig's book *The Art of the Theatre*.

In 1920 Copeau's nephew, Michel Saint-Denis (1897-1971), joined his uncle's Vieux-Colombier company. Undertaking the most menial of tasks, he worked his way up through the ranks and eventually became general-secretary - effectively Copeau's right-hand man. Saint-Denis wrote 'My uncle had realised that the essence of theatre is not  literary, but ritualistic and physical. He wanted to return to the sources: to achieve this purity and to enable the work of a creative ensemble, Copeau created a bare stage, *le tréteau nu*. The whole stage was an acting area, in contrast to that *box of illusions* – the proscenium stage'.

James Agate: The company, by now known as Les Copiaus, had been together since 1924 under Jacques Copeau, mainly, to their frustration, working on studio exercises - although they had been seen at the Cambridge Festival Theatre in 1928 with a touring production of Copeau's *L'Illusion*.

Marius Goring (then 16) was in the audience: 'I'd never seen anything like it; the entire movement of the company was wonderful. I remember Copeau sitting on the steps of the theatre inviting the children on to the stage. And there was a young man, running and waving the mask of an animal's head, shouting *Jouons la comedie*. That was Michel Saint-Denis. One day, I thought, I'll join that company'.
He got his chance six years later.

In June 1929, expecting an appointment to the Comedie-Francaise, Copeau disbanded the company, but they regrouped under Saint-Denis with another change of name to *Compagnie des Quinze*. His *monastic dedication* to his theatrical ideals was no less fanatical than that of his uncle. Believing that the company needed a house author, Saint-Denis contracted André Obey who developed a specialised repertory written specifically for the personalities and playing style of the troupe.

With the *Compagnie des Quinze* Obey found actors who, in in the view of Saint-Denis, were capable of *showing* life rather than *explaining* it, relying more on sound and physical movement than on talking. They were used to singing and dancing, and able to build up from choral work to the invention of simple, clearly-defined characters.

Their first London visit was in 1930 with *Noé*. According to Irving Wardle 'Bronson Albery had seen them in Paris, and backed his fancy by bringing the Compagnie des Quinze to the Arts Theatre, later transferring them to the Ambassadors, and then to the New Theatre: they were a smash. It was not the texts so much as their playing style: the Quinze were acrobats, mimes and musicians whose work enlarged the whole definition of acting'.

They returned in 1932 and 1933, and acquired a tremendous following among that generation of artists then heirs-apparent to the British stage.
Tyrone Guthrie takes up the story: 'Glen Byam Shaw, George Devine, Olivier, myself and many others fell under the spell of Saint-Denis. Gielgud's *Merchant of Venice* at the Old Vic was heavily influenced by the Compagnie des Quinze productions of *Noé*, *La Bataille de la Marne* and *Le Viol de Lucrèce*.

All who saw them were enchanted by their style, the elegance and simplicity of the setting, the choreography, the music of the speech, and especially by the complete break with a naturalism which was already becoming irksome. They played in French, and it was like a delightful spoken opera except that the performers were agile and imaginative. It was like a ballet, only it had fifty times more content than any ballet ever seen. It was like a glamorous but rather *passé* woman in a big shady hat and heaps of tulle'.

Irving Wardle again: 'The Quinze functioned as a team in total opposition to the star hierarchy. London was renewing contact with true ensemble, and the forgotten art of pantomime. They travelled with a light-weight collapsible rostrum and a tent-like surround which did away with the need for wings and which could be packed into a single hamper. This was no mere economy but an expression of their contempt for ordinary theatrical illusion. They could invoke anything they wished without wading into what they called *the mud of naturalism*. For a village they used some miniature roofs and a toy steeple set upon poles. When Lucrece was seen spinning wool with her maidens they presented a picture composed with the care of a Florentine painting, but they did not bother to supply needle and thread. The style was not anti-realistic, but it took off from where realism came to an end'.

In the 1934 dollar crisis all but three members left the Compagnie. Saint-Denis embarked on a fresh plan centred on a large country house near Aix-en-Provence: a new troupe, with classes for summer school students. Among the newcomers were Marius Goring and Vera Poliakoff (later

Vera Lindsay). George Devine (*right*) wrote to Marius Goring. 'You lucky devil. Theatre here is utterly depressing. How I envy you'.
The envy was wasted: the finances in Aix-en-Provence were equally desperate.

At the end of February 1935 Saint-Denis (who spoke virtually no English) came to London to direct John Gielgud in *Noah* at the New Theatre. Despite a cast of *Quinze* disciples including Alec Guinness, Jessica Tandy, Marius Goring and a good supporting company, the magic was missing. 'It was the same lady but seen in a cold, hard north-east light, a raincoat but no hat'.

Saint-Denis and George Devine met for the first time at the start of rehearsals for *Noah*. Two pipe-smokers, each combining acute intellect with a peasant stolidity: they shared a prodigious capacity for hard work, an artisan's sense of craftsmanship, and an agreement over the kind of theatre they wanted. Fortunately, Devine spoke French.

Alec Guinness as the wordless Wolf said that he was driven mad by *Michel's meticulous little moves.* Gielgud admitted that, apart from humming The Sailor's Hornpipe while he hammered the Ark, every detail in the performance was laid down by Saint-Denis, who reproduced *Noah* move by move from the Quinze prompt book.

Although the theatre community clearly appreciated his teaching and directing – Margaret Harris wrote of 'an excitement and character that was unique and thrilling' - the critical community of the time were less enthusiastic, even for a production of *Three Sisters* with John Gielgud, Peggy Ashcroft, Michael Redgrave, Gwen Francon-Davies and George Devine - considered by some to be *the first to bring out the humour of Chekhov's drama.*

Like his uncle in WW1, Saint-Dennis signed up for military service at the start of WW2. He was evacuated from Dunkirk in 1940, and worked with the BBC during the rest of the war transmitting a regular programme *Les*

Francais parlent aux Francais. After the war he formed the Old Vic Studio with George Devine and, in 1945, directed Olivier in *Oedipus Rex* at the Old Vic.

He was part of the triumvirate (with Peter Hall and Peter Brook) heading the new Royal Shakespeare Company, and directed *The Cherry Orchard* during their first season at the Aldwych. Sadly, being stuck in the lighting control box, I barely made contact with Saint-Denis, *Monsieur le Directeur* of my first-ever Chekhov production.

The strong cast was led by Sir John Gielgud and Dame Peggy Ashcroft.

I enjoyed it. Apparently Judi Dench didn't: I should have asked her why: it might have been relevant to this chapter. During his years with the Royal Shakespeare Company Saint-Denis had several roles and titles and responsibilities, mainly involved with the training of actors. His title from 1966 was Consultant Director.

Peter Daubeny's *My World of Theatre* reminds us that uncle Jacques Copeau was not the only director in Paris opening up stages and 'taking theatre to the masses'. In 1951 Jean Vilar, director of the Theatre National Populaire, 'stripped the Palais de Chaillot stage of footlights and battens, and extended it into the auditorium to create a more flexible platform, with an atmosphere *as intimate as music hall.*

'Lighting' he said 'was more important than scenery'. Costumes used strong blocks of colour without unnecessary details; considerable use was made of music and sound. He slashed seat prices; introduced a repertoire of plays *from Moliere to Brecht*, and brought in performers from the cinema – attracting audiences who had previously never set foot in a legitimate theatre.

CHAPTER NINE
LILIAN BAYLIS, QUEEN OF THE OLD VIC

My extensive collection of theatre books includes a wonderful little quarter-bound edition of Edwin Fagg's *The Old Old Vic* – a glimpse of the theatre from its origin as The Royal Coberg, first managed (from 1818) by William Barrymore, through to its revival under Emma Cons and Lilian Baylis.

'From the coming of Waterloo Station in 1840' wrote Fagg, 'the district not only grew, but grew worse. The neighbourhood of Stamford Street housed both ordinary unsavoury criminals and infamous, notorious criminals, as well as pickpockets and thieves of the meaner sort. The attempt to saddle the Vic with the odium and responsibility for its setting, would be as ridiculous as to accuse Waterloo Station of vicious intent'.

However, the Royal Coburg/Royal Victoria Palace had lost its liquor licence, and had become The Victoria Coffee and Music Hall – or what we now know as The Old Vic.

Lilian Baylis was born in London 9th May 1874; daughter of a baritone and a contralto/pianist. She was taught to play violin by John Tiplady Carrodus, and she developed a love for opera. She went to South Africa, taught music, managed a Ladies' Orchestra – and was then summoned home to help her aunt, Emma Cons with the management of the Vic. The Vic had re-opened on Boxing Day 1880 managed first by a Mr Bullock, and later by William Poel until he left to join Frank Benson's company.

Lilian Baylis had *found her tambourine*. She started with Opera performances and only later, in 1914, added some Shakespeare with seasons directed, first by Matheson Lang, and then by Ben Greet (who, as a child, had been prohibited by his parents from attending performances at the *disreputable* Old Vic).

Richard Findlater's book about Lilian Baylis, *The Lady of the Old Vic* is wonderfully comprehensive, but for me the most charming insights by far are in a little 1938 volume from Chapman & Hall, a very personal *tribute to the most courageous woman that was ever associated with the theatre* written by Sybil and Russell Thorndike.

Sybil's brother, Russell Thorndike: 'At the Royal Victoria Hall and People's Coffee Tavern the local inhabitants could see for tuppence a mellow variety of performances, while in the intervals they were encouraged to stimulate themselves with penny cups of coffee. No intoxicants were served, for the *disreputable* theatre had lost its licence. Twice a week they enjoyed opera, not so much for the music as the story – devouring the *book of words* over their coffee and then booing the villains and applauding the hero and heroine'. Matheson Lang proposed a Shakespeare season: she had no money to spend on Shakespeare: *you must make do with the opera props or bring your own*. Lang brought his own, which were almost immediately appropriated by the opera company.

Sybil picks up the story: 'My brothers Russell and Frank were already serving in Egypt, and my husband Lewis (Casson) said I've got to be in this; it will be a war to finish war for ever and he enlisted the next day.

Ben Greet replaced Matheson Lang. Sybil's youngest son John was just getting over scarlet fever when she got a letter from Ben Greet saying 'There's a strange woman running a theatre in the Waterloo Road, Lilian Baylis; you'd find her exciting, Syb, because she's as mad as you are. We're doing *Comedy of Errors* week after next, and I've told her you'll be wonderful as Adriana'. Lilian set the mood at their first meeting: *Well, you won't get much pay, dear, but you'll like the work*, speaking with that twist in the mouth that everyone imitates when repeating her priceless remarks. We did a play a week that autumn, four or five shows a week, and she was right about the pay – ten bob a show'.

Sybil wrote to Russell: *Miss Baylis is an absolute scream. I used to think Miss Horniman the oddest person we had ever worked for: not any more. She talks about 'mucky old Shakespeare' and I simply adore her. She runs the place exactly as people organise parish rooms. She's high church, untidy, and works all hours.*
'Lilian asked me if I'd like to play Lady Macbeth: I'd never played tragedy, but I said I'd love to. She couldn't understand why we made a fuss over these great parts; to her they were just human beings. *She's just trying to get her husband to the top of the tree, that's all: you'd do the same for Lewis'* (who, by then, had departed for France).

William Poel had produced the first *Everyman* in London: The religious subject appealed to Lilian Baylis's instinctive Catholicism and the Old Vic revived it every Lent: Sybil said *Everyman* was one of the few plays which Miss Baylis actually watched all the way through. 'We used Poel's beautiful Elizabethan ideas: in his view, since the coming of the proscenium arch and footlights, we have degenerated from that *living theatre where actors and auditors both partake in the rite and are an integral part of each other'*.

Sybil missed the last play of the season, *Julius Caesar*, as another baby was on the way: three days after the birth Lilian arrived at the cottage with Ophelia's script.

'When can you rehearse, dear? With this baby arriving after the proper time we're running late with *Hamlet*'. Sybil rejoined them a month later, sharing a dressing room about twice the size of a telephone box with Beatrice Wilson and their Elizabethan dresses. Lewis came home on leave when the baby, Ann, was about four months old, and met Lilian for the first time – the start of a long, close friendship.

Russell met her in 1916 when he was invalided out of the army. He was seriously injured in Greece when a machine gun fell on him, dislocating his spine, and he came home an old man, bent nearly double. Recovering slowly at the vicarage, he was visited by Lilian: *you're a crock, you can't fight any more: we want more men so you'd better come and play at the Vic with Sybil.* She told him that she believed in Love and God, and that without them she could not run her Old Vic. Ben Greet wanted her to do *Henry V* but needed men – difficult to find in wartime – so she prayed to God (rather like calling Him on the telephone) asking for *some good actors – cheap.* When Robert Atkins and Andrew Leigh were called up Lilian had the ladies playing men's roles; 'You won't mind, Sybil, will you? After all there should be no sex in acting – you ought to be able to understand men as well as women'.

The Old Vic was the only theatre in London that did consistently good plays all through the war. Arthur Thorndike, father of Sybil and Russell (and a cannon of Rochester Cathedral) and his friend Mr Gordon, vicar of St John's were regulars in the audience: They compared Lilian Baylis to a parish priest when she went before the curtain every week making wonderful speeches begging for money.

Sybil again: 'Granville-Barker came to see *Richard III* and *King Lear*. We were all thrilled – he was a kind of God to many of us. Those of us who worked under him would have followed him anywhere in the theatre. He could have had a company of actors wanting only the bare necessities of living for the joy of working under his direction.

After *my poor fool* was dead that night I went up into the box with him and Lewis – both soldiers on leave. 'You work too hard on stage' Barker said. 'Don't do it from the outside – live inside – it's all there in the play if you just live, and be'. Lilian said much the same, but in her own way: 'These parts are all very easy, you've only got to *be* people, and you know them all – just *be* them'. Queer woman, Miss Baylis. I don't think she knew anything about these plays, but she had something. The next *Macbeth* coincided with my brother Frank's leave, and he played young Siward: his last role – he was killed shortly afterwards. Lilian said 'Wasn't it lovely for him to have been able to act in such a beautiful play before he went'.

In 1918, during a revival of *School for Scandal*, Mr Cochrane, the impresario, was in the audience, and engaged me for a show at the Pavilion. Lilian, like a mother, pushed me out of the nest; 'Out you go' she said. 'Learn something new elsewhere'. She came to the Pavilion to see the show: 'Nice to see you in a pretty frock', she said. Before I left the Vic they did a revue at which Queen Mary and Princess Mary were present. Lilian surpassed herself: having accompanied the Queen to the Royal Box (and calling her 'Dear') she said 'I can't stop here, you know, I've got to go and see all those bounders behind the scenes get on with the job'. Apparently Queen Mary took her hand and said 'Now you sit quietly with me for a minute; they'll get on quite well without you'. For once someone was mothering Lilian.

During the run of *St Joan* I realised what knowing Lilian meant to me. There was a kinship between the peasant saint and Lilian. One thinks of saints in terms of church windows and expressions of conventional godliness. Bernard Shaw realised what is meant by a saint – one who has a vision of God and the work she is called to do; no thought of self – just a shouldering of a burden with never-ceasing courage; never sitting down and saying 'I've done enough', asking nothing for herself – how alike these two were, Joan and Lilian.

Saints must be removed from us by time before we realise they are saints, and Joan must have been as insistent – as irritating – as impossible in her demands as Lilian was. 'She was miraculous – and she was unbearable' said GBS of the Saint, but that was also true of Lilian Baylis'.

Technically, her stage still operated with wing flats slotted into 'grooves' screwed to the stage at the base, and suspended grooves above. The canvas flats were ancient, probably built in the days of Phelps. The footlights were electric, but the battens were still gas. The whole set-up was dangerous, and dirty – but Miss Baylis had other priorities, and would not bother God with requests for the wherewithal to scrap the grooves or install a fully-electric lighting system. Finding actors was a priority: men were in such short supply that even the aged and infirm could demand a salary in the West End, so were not available to the Old Vic. The actresses had to *put on beards* and play male roles. The London County Council at last compelled the removal of the gas battens, and Ben Greet took the opportunity to remove the grooves at the same time.

God offered no direct answer, but the Vicar of St Johns was on the Board of Governors and agreed that the grooves were in the way. Work started at six in the morning: the last one came down just as Miss Baylis arrived for work. She was then faced with raising the money for new scenery, the electric lighting installation, and their own stock of costumes (they had previously hired the majority of costumes from Raynes).

In the opinion of Tyrone Guthrie the decade from 1914 to 1924 didn't just establish the Old Vic (which by then had produced every Shakespeare play in the First Folio) but created the *Old Vic Audience* - serious and predominantly young working people from all over London; intelligent but poor, and consequently unspoiled. However, by the end of the 1920s both the opera and drama companies had expanded beyond the limits of a single building. God commanded Miss Baylis to buy another theatre.

Sadler's Wells Theatre, in Islington had been made famous by Samuel Phelps in the mid-nineteenth century, but was dilapidated to the extent that the stage timbers were dampened by the New River which flowed under the building. She bought it for a song, refurbished it, and opened in 1930 with a gala performance of *Twelfth Night* and a crippling debt.

Sadler's Wells became the home for the opera company, and a ballet company under Edris Stannus – probably better known by her stage name, Ninette de Valois. Two years later Lilian appointed Tyrone Guthrie director of the drama company at the Old Vic: he controversially engaged Charles Laughton (who had never played Shakespeare) to lead a company which included Flora Robson, Athene Seyler, Ursula Jeans, Leon Quartermaine, Roger Livesey and a young James Mason.

Guthrie's production style followed Poel and Barker and Shaw, with no cuts in the script to suit 'the exigencies of stage carpenters', and no scenery except a structure offering the facilities of 'the Elizabethan theatre'. This structure was designed by an architect, proclaimed itself *almost impertinently* to be 'modern', and proved *heavy to manipulate* and *wildly obtrusive*. Painted pinky-grey for the opening production (yet another *Twelfth Night*) it suggested not Illyria but 'a fancy dress ball on a pink battleship'. By the time they reached *Measure for Measure* and *Macbeth* Guthrie had learned how to light and use the set, and it became less obtrusive. Saving money on the sets meant that Miss Baylis could spend her first-ever Pilgrim Trust grant on new costumes – for *stock* – having realised that the *Measure for Measure* costumes would also be suitable for *Rigoletto* at Sadler's Wells.

Macbeth was planned as the high peak of the season. At the dress rehearsal Laughton was electrifying: his performance bore *the unmistakable stamp of genius*. Alas, he never again, except momentarily, fitfully, recovered this greatness.

He lacked technique, and when inspiration failed, as fail it often must, he had very little resource of voice or movement. Miss Baylis, who had not wanted him (yes, but is he a Christian, dear?) went to his dressing room after that first night, caught him a smart crack across the shoulder blades, and said 'Never mind, dear, I'm sure you did your best'.

On First Nights she would *hold court* from her Box, part queen, part showman, but mostly like Lady Bountiful. 'Percy' Harris described how Lilian Baylis sat in the stage box during performances, with her dogs and her cooking  stove, and cooked herself sausages and bacon, with the smell permeating the entire theatre.

John Gielgud thought her 'an extraordinary woman: I never met anybody who knew her really well. The books are quite good about her eccentricities but there's nothing about her professional appreciation of Shakespeare. She had this faith which led her to the people she needed. She went through bombings, and the theatre being destroyed, and moving and opening Sadler's Wells as the home for her opera company - the most adventurous things'.

Lilian Baylis died in 1937, during the *Macbeth* production week which, said Russel Thorndike, in what must have been something of an understatement, *made things difficult*.

The following tributes were among many published in Vic-Wells: the work of Lilian Baylis (1938).

Hugh Walpole: Some saw a saint, some thought her unique, one or two hated her with that vehemence which only remarkable people can arouse, but Lilian's supreme gift was getting other people to perform miracles for her; things that they would never do for anybody else. She has made us feel that the Arts belong to everybody.

Robert Speaight: She had no eye for subtleties of temperament: yet of one thing I am certain: she understood the importance of the actor.
Her most generous praise went to those with an ability to speak Shakespeare's verse. She was naturally, primarily musical, and realised Shakespeare must be music or he is nothing. The genius of this great woman was to understand the mysteries of her subject without waiting on their explanation.

Her secretary Evelyn M Williams: Performing in a Vic-Wells company often led to remunerative offers elsewhere. She went to immense pains to make it possible for artistes to accept these offers, and they knew, and valued, this. The standard she set was always attainable, but never a final one. Neither theatre attempted to run before it could walk, but neither was ever allowed to feel it had attained its maximum speed. As audiences grew so did the standards.

Irene Beeston: Every London theatre was instructed to give a special matinee for War charities. Miss Baylis did not see why, when the artistes and stage and front of house staff were working for nothing, she should have to pay for lighting. 'Write to the electricity people, and tell them that if they deduct the cost of this performance from their bill, I shall be very glad to print that fact on the programme. Tell them that if they don't feel they can let me have the light free, I'll print that too'. The Company was happy to oblige.

Ernest Milton: She had a ruthlessness we all loved. On the telephone to me, at a time when I was not with the company, '(Baliol) Holloway has not recovered from his ankle-sprain: will you play Macbeth tonight?' And one did – having not looked at the part for five years. She could spring the most awful demands on one.

Esme Church: God was so often on her lips, a splendid ally, because He was as real to her as the Chancellor of the Exchequer – and far more reliable.
Perhaps the greatest tribute to her memory is that we remember her not with tears but with affectionate laughter. She would have liked that.

Sumner Austin: She was proud of her CH, her Companion of Honour. She told me that when she received the letter from Prime Minister Lloyd George offering her a DBE she replied 'none of your Dames for me! I don't want to go around the country labelled Dame and be charged double for everything'. The result was the rarer tribute of Companion of Honour. The presentation ceremony was in a room which, she informed us, *is exactly what we want as the setting for Tannhauser*.

Musical Director at Sadlers Wells Laurance Collingwood: She was getting very tired, and worried about how we should carry on without her. She often said to me 'I wish I could die, but what is the good? Who is going to carry on if I go?' Happily she was spared for just those few extra years which enabled her to see her work securely rooted, and that worst of anxieties – the indifference of the public to her enterprise – lived down. She will long be remembered as a great pioneer of Opera, Drama and Ballet in England.

CHAPTER TEN
THE 'ART' OF THE THEATRE

In 1929 Lilian Baylis had appointed Harcourt Williams as Director of the Old Vic: one of his first changes was to sneak a couple of non-Shakespearian works – Moliere's *Imaginary Invalid* and Shaw's *Androcles and the Lion* - into the schedules. He also tightened up the production style: swift, simple changes of scene, adherence to the text and, above all, *pace, pace, pace and pace*. His influences were Poel (clean, fast-paced action); Granville-Barker (direction); Ellen Terry (verse-speaking); and Edward Gordon Craig (design).

Craig was the illegitimate son of actress Ellen Terry, and he worked as an actor in Henry Irving's company off and on until 1897.

In *The Index to the Story of my Days* Edward Gordon Craig (1872-1966) wondered if it had been bad taste to write of himself by spontaneously adding bits of autobiography to his many books on woodcuts, on Irving, on his mother and on theatres. 'I am eighty-five', he continued, 'the age when one can look at oneself and consider one's defects – that is to say, if one has any'.

Being only eighty-one I have had less time to consider my defects – if I have any – but I trust that the 'bits of autobiography' less spontaneously incorporated within this volume will similarly not be considered 'bad taste'.

In his book *The Theatre of Edward Gordon Craig*, the French theatre specialist Dennis Bablet wrote 'Craig's personality, ideas and achievements have always given rise to vehement and conflicting opinions. But since, whether one likes it or not, his influence is to be found everywhere, one should try, as objectively as possible, to define his position in the history of the modern theatre'. So, with Bablet's help, let's try.

Craig was, apparently, a capable actor: Ellen Terry (who may perhaps have been understandably prejudiced) had *never known anyone with so much natural gift for the stage,* and Shaw wanted him for *You Never Can Tell* - but was turned down. Craig also toured and did seasons for other managements.

He planned to marry Helen (May) Gibson daughter of his parents' former neighbour in St Albans, but his mother and Irving (his godfather) both had *reservations*: why is not quite clear. His mother knew he was also friendly with Lucy Wilson and with Jess Dorynne, actresses in other theatre companies: Irving might have known of other *friendships* within the Lyceum company. The marriage went ahead, Easter week 1893 (at that time theatres closed during Holy Week), and May was soon pregnant. Although the couple hardly ever lived together they finished up with four children.

Craig had *significant friendships* with William Nicholson who taught him the art of making wood-cuts, and James Pryde who, he claimed, 'was a joy to  be with but never showed me how to do anything' – despite the evident influence of Pryde's architectural pictures on his future theatre designs.

To support his wife and daughter Craig toured with the W S Hardy Shakespeare Company, playing Hamlet and Romeo. Biographer Michael Holroyd suggests that he was happier as Hamlet *having known no Juliets in his life.* Holroyd hints that Craig did not much enjoy love-making on stage, and even received cat-calls from the audience for his efforts. He went home for the birth of his son Henry (known as Bobby), and then went off on tour again with a company which included Lucy Wilson.

Craig and Lucy went everywhere together but she refused to 'have an affair' with a married man. 'I was still utterly puzzled by the problem of sex; I saw no solution' wrote Craig. His mother couldn't help with either money or advice: 'Don't live with anybody, male or female, unless you go back to Helen and the lovely babies' was her response.

After 1897 Craig developed a stronger interest in design and production. According to Bablet, Craig's first full theatrical production, Purcell's *Dido and Aeneas* 'was a considerable success in London'. *Considerable success* was perhaps a slight exaggeration: after several months of rehearsals with 'some eighty performers' of whom only the soprano and tenor were professionals they staged three performances at the Hampstead Conservatoire. Costs were £379; takings £377. Neither Craig (producer/designer) nor a new *significant friend* Martin Shaw (musical director) drew salaries. Only after their second production together – *Acis and Galatea* in 1902 - did Craig admit that *publicity struck me as something to consider more carefully*.

To live more cheaply Craig and Martin Shaw rented a house on Devonshire Hill; two rooms each, and sharing kitchen etc. and garden. Martin had the upper floor – and the piano. Eventually the arrival of a bailiff forced a 'moonlight flit'.

However, the Hampstead Conservatoire's *empty space* had given Craig the opportunity to develop scenic styles he had first seen in the Bavarian artist Hubert von Herkomer's little theatre at Bushey. Back at the Conservatoire, Craig built a proscenium arch using a scaffolding framework which incorporated lighting towers (complete with platforms for the *lime* operators) but used no wings, no borders, no footlights. Behind side-lit gauzes, great blue and grey sky-cloths went up 'far out of sight' giving (for the first time, some said) a sense of space on the stage. W B Yeats wrote of Craig's purple-lit backcloth 'which had Dido and Aeneas wandering on the edge of eternity'.

Craig put his ideas into print in his own monthly theatre journal *The Mask*, and in a series of books, the best-known of which is *The Art of the Theatre (1905)*, pleading for 'unity of production under one man' and asserting that this director would be the 'true artist of the theatre'. He controversially suggested that 'actors were no more important than marionettes', but later qualified this: *the uber-marionette is an actor plus fire, but minus egotism*: 'the fire of the gods and demons, without the smoke and steam of mortality'. He believed that a director should approach a play with no preconceptions and he embraced this in his 'fading up from the minimum' or *blank canvas* approach to both designing and directing.

My National Theatre colleague, associate director William Gaskill, had little sympathy with Craig's ideas, feeling that his rejection of humanism – *theatre should be made of images; literary theatre is dead; away with narrative and linear thinking* - left no place for the writer, although he agreed with Craig's expressed hopes for 'a school where the art of the theatre might be studied in all its aspects'. The theatre, Craig thought, unlike literature, painting, music, 'had no standards: it lived from hand to mouth, from season to season, at the mercy of the whims of theatrical promoters following ephemeral fashions of the personal ambitions or predilections of actor-managers'.

Peter Brook believed Craig to be 'more important than Brecht, Meyerhold, Stanislavsky or Artaud in the sense that he was at the origin of it all, although never truly honoured in his own country (*within the theatre community, Brook presumably meant, since Craig was publicly awarded an OBE, and later made a Companion of Honour, the same recognition accorded Lilian Baylis*).

Isadora Duncan, with whom Craig had a long affair (and a daughter) introduced him to Konstantin Stanislavsky, the founder of the Moscow Arts Theatre, leading to an invitation to direct *Hamlet* there. This, the production for which Craig is best-remembered, eventually opened in December 1911, and was reviewed by Kaoru Osanai, a visiting Japanese Theatre Director:

'This *Hamlet* had no cut-out trees, no painted canvas, no sculptured pillars, no arched ceiling. Everything there was represented by screens. These could be folded many times to the desired width, and furthermore each piece was made detachable. Thus, the screens could be made into a corridor which could turn diagonally, a wall which could stand up straight or pillars which could stand apart from each other.

The staging consisted only of a group of straight lines running parallel to the stage and another group of straight lines crossing the stage at a right angle. Craig painted one side of the screens cream and the other gold so that he could reverse them when he desired. The cream was always employed for an outdoor scene, the exterior of a building, the house of Polonius, etc.

The interior of the Elsinore palace was always presented in gold. When the gold was employed, a wide beam of strong light was thrown downward from the ceiling crossing the space diagonally.

It never lighted up the whole stage with dazzling brightness - if I try to explain it in a familiar Japanese scene, it will be the morning sunbeam which peeps into the dark kitchen through the skylight, just as a wide beam of light, with the rest of the setting only vaguely seen in the golden reflection. The intention was to create the effect of tarnished gold.

The colour of the costumes was also softened. Even though the king, the queen, and the courtiers all wore costumes which had a woven design of golden thread, the thread was pliable and tarnished. The costumes for Hamlet and Horatio were of a colour between blue and indigo. We could see the high steps at the centre. At the top of the steps we saw the large, smooth, semi-circular back of a chair which was painted gold. On this chair the king and queen sat wearing gold crowns and gold attire. From the foot of the chair downward a great number of courtiers filled the wide steps. Their costumes were also done in gold. When the curtain was raised, it revealed an almost perfect sculpture of a crowd, presenting the beautiful composition of the king and queen sitting on the chair and the courtiers standing on both sides. The crowd in the sculpture did not move at all for some time. I was so impressed that I felt as if I were observing a great sculptor employing his chisel with exacting skill and unrelenting concentration'.

Craig was also innovative in his use of stage lighting: colour and light were central to his stage conceptions. He did away with the footlights, and lit his stages from above, placing lights in the ceiling of the theatre. Osanai wrote of 'the background becoming a deep shimmering blue, apparently almost translucent, upon which the green and purple make a harmony of great richness'. For the church scene in his mother's production of *Much Ado About Nothing* Craig had a *strong ray of sunlight falling on the stage in a thousand colours through an invisible stained-glass window*. All this use of vivid colour comes as a shock if, like mine, your own most familiar illustrations of Craig's designs are the woodcuts and the simple black-and-white sketches of his brutalist 'blocks'.

What a difference a bit of colour makes . . .

West End producer Frith Banbury: 'Sets and lighting were primitive until more imaginative people such as Rex Whistler and George W Harrison (Basil Dean's designer) came along.

One of the most imaginative was Gordon Craig: he lived abroad, didn't like the English theatre, and introduced the idea of a *unified stage picture* that covered all the elements of design - but most of his work was done in influential books, very little actually in the theatre'. He produced nothing in England after *The Vikings, (right)* in 1903.

His work before that date had influenced Max Reinhardt at the Deutsches Theater, where realistic presentation gave way to symbolic and decorative sets with colourful lighting. *Craigische Vorstellung* became an accepted production style, and added an adjective to the German language.

Craig, an Outsider, preferred living in France or Italy: Ashley Dukes visited him in his Genoese villa, 'entering a room so full of books that they covered the walls. Craig' he thought, 'was mistrusted by his countrymen as only a man can be who writes as well as he draws, and talks as well as either; who never concealed his revolutionary aims in theatre design and practice, and yet acquired a name as well known in Europe as Stanislavsky or Appia'. He had lately produced Ibsen's *The Pretenders* in Copenhagen'. Craig lived in straitened circumstances in France for much of his life and was interned by German Occupation forces in 1942. He died at <u>Vence</u>, France, in 1966, aged 94.

I read some of Craig's books over fifty years ago, and took a great deal from them; particularly his thought that every production should have a dominant central design feature – usually seeking such a feature in my own productions.

My suspicion is that Craig's *neglect,* his lack of commissions, were largely his own fault: he was offered directing and design opportunities in several European countries, but invariably delayed decisions and designs, and was replaced – or productions were simply cancelled. Craig was considered extremely difficult to work with and ultimately refused to direct or design any project over which he did not have complete artistic control. This led to his withdrawal from practical theatre production and his later career is remarkable for how little he achieved after the age of forty, during a long period of over fifty years.

Before moving on, we should perhaps mention one other scene designer of this period: a man in complete contrast to Craig. He was busy; he was successful, and he was in a life-long settled home relationship with his partner Charles Shannon. He was the artist, publisher and stage designer Charles Ricketts (1866-1931), equally popular with both the commercial and independent managements, having designed sets and costumes for Shaw's *St Joan* as well as for the D'Oyle Carte *Mikado.* When *Don Juan in Hell* was produced at the Court for a series of matinees, Charles Ricketts designed costumes in the style of Velasquez. Lillah McCarthy remembered that hers was 'glorious, rose silk covered in black lace and silver trimming, with a flame feather in my hair'.

Ricketts was inspired and delighted by working with Shaw, but the association between them seemed to end sadly: reaching the summit of his career with the sets and costumes for *St Joan,* Ricketts found a changed Shaw.

'Shaw's little lectures in the wings and exaggerated renderings of what he wanted used to be delightful' Ricketts remembered. 'Today he only thinks of his *points* and, I believe, dislikes good acting and production'. Lillah was devoted to Shaw, and believed in his genius, but found herself asking 'Is Ricketts right?' Shaw was approaching seventy. We all get tired more easily, tetchy even, as we get older. Why should Shaw have been any different?

Who, then, are the designers I best remember from my own working days?

I would put Peter Rice near the top of my list.  His designs were original, practical and always within budget. He was pleasant to work with, and totally understood that if he didn't leave space for the lights then his work would not be seen to the best advantage. You would think that was common sense, even common practice: sadly, it wasn't. His first designs were three 1956 Shakespeare productions for Michael Benthall during that period when the Old Vic was re-staging all of the plays in the First Folio. Ten years later I worked with Peter at Scottish Opera on his very formal, almost *Craigian* central open tower setting for *Faust*, and then a more traditional pastel Elizabethan set for *Falstaff*. The one that really impressed me, though, was an ingenious, multi-level staging for *La Bohème* providing three totally different pictures, but involving relatively simple interval changes. Scottish Opera in those days was a wholly-touring company: the sets had to be practical, and Peter's always were.

I got to know him better when we were both involved on an opera double bill at the Cheltenham Music Festival: a tight budget, so we were making and painting the sets in the wings of the Everyman Theatre. Again, the designs were both appropriate and 'practical'. I don't remember him ever overdoing his designs in order to get 'noticed, or taking advantage of a bigger-than-usual budget (why does the National Theatre suddenly come to mind?).

I didn't see any of his sets for the 1966 season at the Chichester Festival Theatre, but Alan Strachan was full of praise for his work there. It's not an easy stage for set or lighting designers. Or, indeed, for actors, directors or audiences: Richard Briers famously said that to get a laugh on the thrust stage at Chichester you had to act like Grock.

Of the contemporary designers, I find the work of Lez Brotherston particularly exciting. He was a Peter Rice student and came to notice (for me, anyway) with his amazing (and amazingly-practical) designs for Matthew Bourne. I love most of his work; it is personal and original, yet always perfectly complements the varying styles of his directors/choreographers and their productions. His designs for a revival of *Oh What a Lovely War* (a show I know better than most) was in total contrast to John Bury's original, but still perfectly suited the period and the style.

I only worked with Ralph Koltai twice: first was the RSC *Caucasian Chalk Circle* at the Aldwych when I remember two huge walls dominating what might otherwise have been a lighter, fast-moving production. On the second occasion he squeezed an enormous metal set onto our Stratford East stage for a two-week try-out of a new (hopefully) commercial production. Even I could see that the set was too solid for such a rickety play: I asked him why he had done it, and he replied that it was his policy to design ever more dominating sets 'until they talk about me the same way they talk about Sean Kenny'.

Sean Kenny's brief spell of success almost exactly corresponded with the London part of my career, and for the same reason: the mass production of spotlights (or *lanterns* or *luminaires* depending on which gang you hung around with). This made them cheap enough for theatres to be able to purchase them in quantity, and position them all around the stage as well as out in the auditorium, allowing us to 'shape' the lighting – coming at the scenery and performers from all angles and providing that essential *third dimension*.

Until that point we had relied on lighting battens: flat light on to flat canvas backcloths. This new ability to light 'shape' allowed Sean to design those award-winning, three-dimensional lumbering wooden sets for *Oliver!*. The need to control each of these many spotlights independently led to the more intricate control panels such as those at the Comedy and Aldwych theatres which took me into the West End.

In 1959 Sean designed the Mermaid's opening show *Lock Up Your Daughters*; in 1960 he designed *The Hostage* for Joan Littlewood (*right*). I was with the RSC in 1961 when he designed *The Devils*. For the National Theatre at the Old Vic Sean designed the opening production *Hamlet,* and was  also involved in the transformation of the theatre's stage. Along with the rest of a huge technical crew I virtually lived on his massive three–dimensional metal sets for Lionel Bart's

 *Blitz!* - such a complicated set that they rented a cinema in Edmonton, where we spent a month getting the huge metal towers and bridges together, and then doing previews before transferring it to the Adelphi. Lionel attempted to direct it himself; eventually a 'choreographer' was brought in to tighten everything up and give it some shape. At the time of its Adelphi opening on 8th May 1962 it was the most expensive production to go into the West End. Although not universally welcomed (Benedict Nightingale wrote 'Oh what an average war'), it settled in for a longish run. Noel Coward called it 'twice as loud and twice as long as the real thing'. Sean Kenny died in 1973 of a massive heart attack: Peter Roberts, in *Plays and Players*, wrote of Sean: 'His influence is incalculable. His imaginative use of modern theatrical technology paved the way for all the British musical extravaganza which followed'.

John Napier's first-ever set design was for *The Ruling Class* during my time at Nottingham Playhouse. He went on to bigger and ever more expensive productions leading to Richard Eyre's comment in his *Diaries*: 'John Napier, designer of big musicals for Cameron Mackintosh, has designed *Trelawny of the Wells* for the Olivier stage at the National Theatre, and we're having huge budget problems. Years of musicals may have expanded his imagination, but haven't taught him economy'.

Franco Zeffirelli wasn't strong on economy either. During my year with the NT at the Old Vic an exuberant Zeffirelli turned up to direct *Much Ado About Nothing*. Trained by Visconti, he too preferred to design his own sets – in this instance his designs were loosely based on the brightly-coloured Jewish folk art paintings of Chagall.

Two weeks before the opening he returned from Italy with an incredible design for a metal-framed front arch supporting thousands of miniature light bulbs wired into three different-coloured circuits - a different pattern for each circuit. Complex, much too expensive, and impossible to make in the time available. 'So, I go back to Italy' he said with a shrug. It was made, of course, with the Old Vic technicians racing against

time to wire up all the miniature bulbs. It looked stunning, but fed stored up resentment when the *staff directors* wanted some special effect for their own productions later in the season and were denied *because of the budget*. 'Zeffirelli would have got it' they suggested, without success. 'So, I go back to Sloane Square' didn't present quite the same threat.

I was part-exchanged with John Bury at Stratford East, so never actually worked *with* him but his designs and his achievements there were impressive. Having just left the Navy, John started with Theatre Workshop as an actor but found he was of more use as an electrician. His natural progression was to lighting designer, and then set designer. 'I found I could only light sets which I had designed' he admitted. He thought in terms of shapes, materials and textures, knowingly influenced by the Berliner Ensemble's designer, Caspar Neher.

Neher's design for The Good Woman of Setzuan

On the bookshelf nearest to my desk sits a copy of *The Art of the Theatre Workshop* put together by actor/archivist Murray Melvin and published by Oberon Press. A wonderful photographic record of Theatre Workshop's set designs over the years, the majority of them by John Bury. He joined the newly-formed Royal Shakespeare Company as Head of Design in 1960, and then followed Peter Hall to the National Theatre. He returned only once to work at Stratford East, on *Oh What a Lovely War,* and was busy with *The Wars of the Roses* trilogy when *Lovely War* transferred into the West End, which was how I got involved with Joan and her *clowns* (her word for possibly the most successful 'permanent company' ever in the British theatre). More on them later.

John Bury at work on his set for *The Good Soldier Schweik*.

One could probably fill several books with the 'art' of Motley, but their careers (and lives) are so intertwined with actors/directors/managements mentioned in these pages that we should at least introduce them here. Elizabeth Montgomery first met the Harris sisters, Margaret and Sophia, at a Chelsea art school. They made weekend visits to the Old Vic, but were still without practical stage design experience when Gielgud offered them the chance to provide costumes for the Oxford *Romeo and Juliet*. 'He really taught us rather than directed us'.

The (cheap) set was borrowed, but the partners – who saw costume as an integral part of stage character – created stunning effects with the humblest of materials. They proved a well-balanced team: Elizabeth had the imagination and a ravishing sense of colour; Margaret (known as Percy) was the artist/craftsman, specialising in set design; Sophia designed and made costumes, quickly, and in great quantities.

Their first London production was also for Gielgud: two performances of a new play *Richard of Bordeaux* at the Arts Theatre. They designed and made sets and costumes. George Devine, who had moved in with them, helped with the sewing. They rented a derelict third-floor studio in St Martins Lane, a former night club, a venue which became an unofficial club for the acting profession, with a tea bill approaching £100 a week. Gielgud, was one of many regular visitors. Devine became Manager, looking after the business without jeopardising their artistic integrity.

Their big break-through came with Gielgud's 1932 *Merchant of Venice* at the Old Vic. He agreed to direct without a fee if Lilian Baylis paid for newly-designed sets and costumes – by Motley. The £600 bill shocked Miss Baylis but proved to be money well spent, and future Old Vic directors had more freedom (and cash) for new designs. Next came a New Theatre revival of their *Richard of Bordeaux*: Motley's new sets evoked pavilions and cloisters in indigo, cream and rust-red; new costumes were entirely made from wool. The *Bordeaux* first-night party turned the Motley Studios into 'a powerhouse; a meeting place where plans were hatched by rising members of the theatre establishment'.

After the formation of the London Theatre Studio George Devine, already administrator and teacher, added stage manager to his duties. Breuer had put in some lights and, using £600 of his own money, Devine added to that installation, supplied some sound equipment, and began to experiment – to the extent that Marius Goring admitted that from 1937 to 1939 'there was nobody to touch him as a lighter'. Margaret Harris said that he took immense trouble to get the exact colour. The Times listed his 'control of lighting, particularly in the garden scene' among the chief assets of a production of *The Three Sisters*.

CHAPTER ELEVEN
ENTER LEFT: GEORGE DEVINE

So – who was this George Devine? Irving Wardle is best-placed to answer that question having provided a superb biography *The Theatres of George Devine*.

Devine started as a member of OUDS at Oxford, finding early influences in Komisarjevsky's little theatre in Barnes 1925/26. As President of OUDS Devine offered John Gielgud his first opportunity to direct, a production of *Romeo and Juliet* at Oxford's New Theatre in February 1932. Gielgud accepted, happily agreed to cast Christopher Hassall as Romeo, and less-happily agreed *greasy, spotty, unattractive but intelligent* George Devine as Mercutio. He also brought in his own design team (the three young ladies who later became famous as Motley), with Edith Evans to play Nurse. Peggy Ashcroft was Juliet. Gielgud's production style owed something to Harcourt Williams's recent work at the Old Vic (Gielgud had been a member of his company) and much to William Poel and Granville-Barker. A review in The Times calling it 'the best balanced and most satisfying performance of recent years'.

That encouraged Bronson Albery to give the OUDS *Romeo and Juliet* a Sunday night in the West End's New Theatre, with proceeds going to the Old Vic. Terence Rattigan thought Devine was miscast 'but pretty damn good all the same'. Komisarjevsky (married at the time, but not for long, to Peggy Ashcroft) must have agreed, because he offered Devine work in London. When the University reassembled in April, Devine – who should have been preparing for his Finals – was in London rehearsing with Komisarjevsky.

He played small parts under Harcourt Williams's direction at the Old Vic: he moved in with the Motleys – starting a relationship with Sophie Harris which would eventually lead to marriage - and he kept in touch with Gielgud whose dreams of combining the presentational quality of the West End with the dramatic quality of the Old Vic became reality with *The Merchant of Venice* in Motley's sets. Gielgud's revival of *Richard of Bordeaux* at the New Theatre (again with Motley) proved his biggest success to date: Devine remained at the Vic until the end of his contract, then in May 1934 he was at Sadlers Wells for a revival of Barker's *The Voysey Inheritance* directed by Barker himself - who arrived each day incognito in bowler hat and striped trousers, with a Rolls outside the door to rush him back to the Mayfair for lunch *but it was a fantastic experience*. In Barker's view 'for our sort of plays, and our sort of attitude to the theatre, real repertory and a permanent company are the only solution'.

Devine next joined Laurence Olivier and Glen Byam Shaw in Gielgud's production of *Queen of Scots*. They became his lifelong friends, as well as his instructors in the art of stage make-up which Devine had never previously mastered. He also developed his knowledge of sets, lighting and props. The next step up the ladder was another Gielgud production, *Hamlet*, with Devine as the Player King, and a first West End role for Alec Guinness as Osric. Michel Saint-Denis arrived in London to direct Gielgud in an English translation, *Noah*, of the *Quinze* success, Obey's *Noé* in which Devine played the Bear. 'Type-casting' said Gielgud.

Devine's next role was Peter in Gielgud's 1932 *Romeo and Juliet* (with Peggy Ashcroft and Edith Evans), gathering praise and excellent notices, after which he joined with Marius Goring and Saint-Denis in an attempt to form a British version of the *Quinze*. Bronson Albery, Tyrone Guthrie, Charles Laughton, Olivier and Gielgud all offered financial support – but not sufficient to acquire property, so when the London Theatre Studio opened in January1936 it was in a practice room in Beak Street, Diaghilev's old studio. It started as a school 'from which actors of the right kind would emerge'.

Thanks to an anonymous cheque the second term saw them transplanted to Providence Hall, a disused Methodist Chapel in Islington. The intention of the school, as Marius Goring saw it, was not to 'turn out' young actors and actresses able to act in average plays in the West End, but to produce a homogeneous troupe of people working in the theatre, with writers, musicians and mechanics trained to support it. As well as being a school, it was to be a dramatic centre and attract to itself many people who were already in the theatre.

A 22-year-old Alec Guinness advised a young Peter Daubeny 'The only acting school worth training at is the London Theatre Studio', but Daubeny confessed that he hated every moment of the year he spent under Saint-Denis in the 'disused chapel in Islington. It looked like a gymnasium, and its curriculum seemed more suitable for a seminary of psychiatric therapists than students of drama. Day after day we would improvise solemnly on extravagantly bizarre themes: 'now you're a dinosaur in labour', 'now you're a bush in a snowstorm'; 'now you come home to find there's no tea and your mother has been raped'. I suppose it stretched and tested our imagination, but I found it incomprehensible, boring and grotesque, lacking the mystery and excitement of either Stanislavsky's books or, for that matter, of Saint-Denis's own productions then dazzling London – *The Three Sisters,* Bulgakov's *The White Guard* and *Twelfth Night'*.

A fellow-student, Peter Ustinov, travelled on Daubeny's bus each morning, enlivening the ride with graphic interpretations of whatever new fantasies the day might hold in store for them. Saint-Denis once described Ustinov as 'possessing a dangerous facility which would need counteracting with discipline'. Ustinov found 'something withdrawn, more awesome than approachable, about Saint-Denis, 'a father to everyone but no one's friend'. Behind the mask lay kindness and good humour, but I was too inexperienced to absorb the ideas which were to make him a pioneer influence on the British post-war theatre. What I desperately needed, but didn't get, was reassurance'.

A view supported by Yvonne Mitchell: 'We were absolutely untrained for the theatre of the day. Nobody told us how to get a job. Nobody told us how to write to a rep and enclose a stamped addressed envelope. Nobody told us how to speak in drawing room plays. They developed us as inventors and improvisers, but there was no place for us'.

Irving Wardle also appeared to have reservations: 'Before the arrival of Saint-Denis we had ten or fifteen *théâtres de poche*, all very esoteric and highbrow, where theatre was *a serious matter*. It seemed to me that the arrival of Saint-Denis in London merely added yet another esoteric group; in France he had a company but no school: in London he had a school but no company'.

I'm afraid that I share some of Mr Wardle's cynicism. The *Quinze* had been so esoteric that Saint-Denis had to engage André Obey to write pieces to suit their particular style'. I can see why actors might want to attend such a school to widen and develop their talents; to 'stretch themselves', but I have never been able to see it as a major national advancement in dramatic production, particularly when, as Yvonne Mitchell pointed out, the bulk of the students' future opportunities would have been in commercial productions or repertory companies where the *Quinze* style would be of little benefit.

I write this in the full knowledge that the Saint-Denis Supporters Club included many of the 'greats' of that time. Olivier and Peggy Ashcroft trusted Saint-Denis; Guinness and Redgrave claimed that careers were transformed by his influence; for Jocelyn Herbert 'he gave us a sense of direction not only in our work but in our lives' and yet if, at the end of their three years training, Saint-Denis had formed a British company along the lines of *Compagnie des Quinze*, it is highly unlikely that any of the above would have been members. The rewards awaiting them in the West End, Broadway or Hollywood would surely have proved too great an attraction.

None of which stops me nominating George Devine, Saint-Denis' administrator at the London Theatre Studio, as (after Granville-Barker, of course) the man I most regret never having worked with. The opportunity was never on offer; I didn't start in the theatre until 1959, and by the time I had sufficient experience to interest the Royal Court, Devine had died of a massive heart attack. That was in January 1966, during the run of one of the Court's most successful productions, John Osborne's *A Patriot For Me,* featuring Devine as Baron von Epp, 'hostess' at the drag ball. Irving Wardle's excellent biography catches the energy, ability and imagination of George Devine in all branches of the theatre - artistic,  technical and administrative - with which he - and, indeed, I - were involved. I do so wish I had known him, or at least had an opportunity to work with him.

My family moved to Fulham in 1953. I was less than a year away from 'O' levels, so allowed to stay on at Beckenham Grammar which meant a bus ride to Victoria station every morning. The number 11 bus went through Sloane Square, passing the Royal Court Theatre at a time when it was still home to intimate revues such as *Airs on a Shoestring* and *Fresh Airs*, usually directed by Laurier Lister with Max Adrian starring, and casts including the likes of Denis Quilley, Moyra Fraser, Betty Marsden, Rose Hill and Julian Orchard, performing material by such as Flanders and Swann. By the time I finished National Service the English Stage Company had taken up residence at the Court. George Devine reportedly said 'For me, the theatre is really a religion or way of life. Make sure you don't get into the wrong temple. You must decide what the world is about and what you want to say about it, so that everything in your theatre is saying the same thing. If you can't find one you like, start one of your own'. By taking the English Stage Society into the Royal Court George had effectively *found his tambourine*.

Frith Banbury called George Devine *the man who created the Royal Court*. 'He wanted so much to change what he thought was wrong in the theatre. He had an up-to-date-ness, a modern-ness, and he collected good people around him: including a close friendship with the inexperienced-but-talented Tony Richardson which surprised Saint-Denis: his reaction was *I think George is in love*. Devine found the plays, and filled the company with all the most interesting young actors and actresses (as John Gielgud had done) although it must be admitted that few of them had actually studied at the London Theatre Studio or the Old Vic School. Devine refused to 'cheat': never pretended that the stage was anything other than a stage, or the actors anything other than actors'.

His strength was comedy. One of my own earliest cinematic influences was a 1942 black-and-white movie version of Ole Olsen and Chic Johnson's 1938 revue *Hellzapoppin*. 'Zany' said the review, and 'zany' it was: I drew on its humour for one of my earliest stage scripts *Casablanca Here I Come*. I imagine that it also influenced the French director/performer Robert Dhery whose 'masterpiece of organised disaster' *La Plume de ma Tante* had a huge success in London, and which I also saw more than once. George Devine shared my tastes, it seems, because after seeing *La Plume de ma Tante* he admitted, wistfully, 'I've wanted to do that all my life'.

In fact, he did do something similar during a final year show at the Old Vic School, as Irving Wardle describes: 'Amid the applause for a cut version of *All's Well that Ends Well* the curtain sailed up and got stuck, revealing the stage crew striking the set. Spotting the audience, they disappeared with a warning yell. Frantic off-stage dispute, and back they came to do a double-quick set-change into *The Clandestine Marriage* to a silent-film-style piano accompaniment. The set then started fighting back. Maladroit stage hands were left clinging to the tops of flats; others got stranded on the stage bars which took off to the fly-tower and then went up and down like yo-yos with the terrified victims doing Harold Lloyd plank-walking feats.

Two of them let go of a flat and then just caught it as it was falling out towards the audience. A clearing stick just missed a fouled chandelier and knocked one of the crew off a step-ladder. Someone nailing down a piece of scenery nailed his trousers to the stage, ripping off one leg when he stood up. Enter numerous figures carrying flats over the stage; half-way across a figure walking downstage vanished into the mobile maze and was fitfully glimpsed desperately signalling through gaps in the passing scenery. Meanwhile a personal feud had developed between the slow-witted fly-man and the bossy head carpenter, reaching its climax with the fly-man's triumphant shout 'I've fixed the curtain' whereupon the curtain fell, carrying his enraged adversary up to the flies by his belt'.

The whole thing was over in ten minutes, leaving the stage set for the next item. To which I can only comment 'I've wanted to do that all my life'.

'Mere technique is useless' Devine told one class, echoing Copeau: 'a *sense of theatre* is as vital to technicians as it is to performers. With it, the curtain can be made to act as much as any actor, and lights can be made to talk as eloquently as any poetry. From the man who works the tabs to the girl who designs the crown for King Lear, each of these people is an artist just as much as the director or designer'.

With details of the Royal Court lease finally agreed, Richardson and Devine could concentrate on the opening programme. They advertised in The Stage for new plays: 750 were submitted, but only one was considered by the two directors – a script from a penniless author living on a houseboat. The play was *Look Back In Anger* and its author was John Osborne. George immediately realised that this was the play which would establish the Royal Court style.

He also appreciated that, because the play would *enlarge the limits of the theatrically-acceptable*, they daren't open the season with it for fear of upsetting the very establishment on which they now depended for patronage – despite the fact that Beckett's *Waiting For Godot* had opened nine months previously, and was still running in the West End.

CHAPTER TWELVE
SHAKESPEARE'S BACK IN TOWN

In 1955 the 24-year-old Cambridge graduate Peter Hall was running the tiny Arts Theatre when Donald Albery offered him the script of *Waiting for Godot* by Samuel Beckett. 'It's been on for some time in Paris in a 75-seat theatre and is highly regarded' said Mr Albery. Peter Hall, who had 'vaguely heard of Beckett, vaguely knew about the play' read it and found it  startlingly original. Waiting as a metaphor for living. Will Godot come? Will something come to explain why we're here and what we're doing? Poetic drama, yet terribly funny, with that extraordinary Irish rhythm. Hard to cast, he thought, but he took it on.

They rehearsed through a hot summer and opened in late August. The drab, almost-bare stage was dominated by a withered tree and a garbage can; a lugubrious setting which  was mainly inhabited by a couple of verminous tramps with sweaty feet, inconstant bladders and boils on their backsides.

There was no action: Vladimir and Estragon were waiting for Godot but, as the audience guessed from the beginning, Godot would never come. When Estragon said 'Nothing happens, nobody comes, nobody goes, it's awful' a voice from the audience responded 'Hear, hear!' Certain early lines, such as 'I have had better entertainment elsewhere', were received with ironical laughter. Most of the critics were bored and outraged by it. The play was quite warmly applauded, but butchered the following morning by the dailies: The Guardian said 'This really won't do'.

Happily, Kenneth Tynan in the Observer, and Harold Hobson in the Sunday Times recognised the quality of Beckett's writing and proclaimed it boldly. Hobson continued his praise over the next six Sundays. Thanks to them, *Waiting for Godot* transferred to the Ambassadors Theatre, ran for over a year, and Beckett's role as a major playwright was established. In Hall's view, 'I don't think that Pinter or Stoppard would have written the way they did – or perhaps not at all – had it not been for Beckett. I would advance the theory that *Godot* is the masterpiece of the mid-century, certainly way, way, way more important than *Look Back in Anger*'.

Well, he would say that, wouldn't he? - the success of *Waiting for Godot* took Peter Hall to Stratford on Avon. And completely transformed his life.

Barry Jackson, previously Director at the Birmingham Rep and the Malvern Festivals, took over as Director of the Stratford Memorial Theatre in 1945 and restored some of the pre-war glamour. He recruited Diana Wynyard, and young Paul Scofield and young Peter Brook and built up an infrastructure of rehearsal rooms, and workshops. His successor Anthony Quayle took over just as Olivier and Richardson departed from the Old Vic, allowing Stratford (in Harold Hobson's words) *to acquire international stature* before handing over to Glen Byam Shaw. However, Stratford seasons ran from March to October – and the burden of re-starting each year with a fresh, star-led company disillusioned even these great directors.

On the strength of his success with *Waiting for Godot* Peter Hall (still only 25) was invited by Byam Shaw to do a production there in 1956, and to return in each of the next two seasons. Glen Byam Shaw retired in 1958 and asked Hall, by then aged 28, if he wanted to take over. Hall's response? 'Of course I did; that was my ambition, but not to take over an *ad hoc* summer Festival. I wanted an ensemble, with the principal players on three-year contracts, all prepared to approach Shakespeare in the same way. With a team of directors and a team of designers, and with a mixed repertoire including both classics and contemporary plays.

A year-round operation, Stratford-based, but with a second theatre in London. I explained the political problem to the Board: within the next five years or so there would be a National Theatre, and Stratford will become just another provincial repertory theatre, visited only by tourists'. 'There can't be two national theatres' they said, but Hall believed that artistic competition was essential, just as France had both the Comedie Francaise and Vilar's Theatre National Populaire. There was strong hostility from some of the Board: Binkie Beaumont resigned, partly over concerns about how the three-year contracts might affect his West End theatrical empire.

Sir Fordham Flower, chairman of the board (and of the Flowers Brewery), was interested, but worried about resources. Apart from a couple of seasons after the war when Barry Jackson was leading its recovery, the Memorial Theatre had always covered its costs thanks largely to Brewery sponsorship, so had never needed to apply for public funding. 'And we'll never get public funding all the time we're covering costs' said Hall, quickly running the company into deficit. In the process he got his year-round operation; his three-year contracts, his team of directors and designers, and his London venue, the Aldwych Theatre – plus an Arts Council grant. 'Without adequate subsidy we cannot develop the means by which our rich dramatic heritage may be kept part of our lives'.

The Stage: 27.10.1961. 'Peter Hall has made theatrical history by planning to engage thirty-five artists for a three-year period to create the nucleus of a Company which is to provide plays in both Stratford and London. A sense of pride might be fostered in such a company – that same pride which one encounters in the Berliner Ensemble, in the Moscow Arts Company, and at the Comédie Francaise. Actors enjoy being one of a company drawing audiences from the four corners of the earth to come and see it – solely on the strength of its name. In recent Stratford seasons one has marvelled at the fluid teamwork after playing together for months on end. Mr Hall's ensemble will be playing together for years on end, and we can expect to enjoy work such as we have rarely seen in an English company'.

Peter Hall created the Royal Shakespeare Company, and provided the template of the modern theatre director – described by one of his successors as part-magus, part-impresario, part-politician, part-celebrity. This 'godfather of modern British theatre' announced his *credo*. The primary building block of the RSC would be the verse: the text to be spoken wittily, trippingly, not singing it, not being pompous, meaning what was said, and thereby exposing the dialectic of the scene. In his view there were about half-a-dozen directors and fifty actors left in England who actually knew how to do Shakespeare; sufficient to pass it on. 'It will swing back again' he said; 'it always does'.

23rd April (Shakespeare's birthday) 1960 saw the opening production of the new Royal Shakespeare Company: *The Merchant of Venice* – as reviewed here by Roger Gellert in the New Statesman: 'All the faults and hesitations, all the  skylarking and parade, were annulled by Peter O'Toole's Shylock. I don't know what it is that suddenly produces, in all the polished adequacy of English acting, a great performance. Whatever that quality is, O'Toole has it. One ingredient, certainly, is authority: the ability to grip an audience by its throat even while speaking slowly and hardly above a whisper. Another is sheer physical presence: like Olivier, O'Toole has an animal magnetism no matter what he is doing or who else is present; for example, while the trial rages around him, he sits deliberately sharpening his knife on his shoe.

He is intent but quiet, not a movement is demonstrative, yet one can't take one's eyes off him. Then there is his intelligence: each word and gesture is thought out and disciplined without for a moment appearing over-rehearsed. These all add up to an inwardness, a certain inward tension: without histrionics, O'Toole imposes on his audience a pressure of emotion and dignity which transforms Shylock from an ambiguous figure hovering somewhere between caricature and melodrama into a major tragic hero'.

The Aldwych would not re-open until December 15th 1960: by then the back-stage technical facilities had been gutted; an apron stage built out over the orchestra pit with staircases each side leading down to the under-stage area.

The stage flying equipment was updated; improved sound and lighting installed – including the new lighting control desk in what had been the lower stage right stalls box, behind a large new plate-glass window. That box would be my workplace, and that window my view of the majority of the company's London performances over the next two years.

The London repertory would consist mainly of non-Shakespearean plays *in which the actors could respond to all the influences of modern and classic drama, and build a bridge between the classical and the popular theatre.* First show in was Webster's *The Duchess of Malfi*, with Dame Peggy Ashcroft in the title role. It introduced us to many of the principal actors and actresses who would grace our stage for the remainder of their three-year contracts including Derek Godfrey, Max Adrian, Eric Porter and Patrick Wymark. Further down the cast list were names that would soon become familiar: Diana Rigg, Roy Dotrice, Sian Phillips, Clive Swift, Tony Church and Ian Holm. One face that was more familiar to me than most was Peter Jeffrey's: he had been Peter O'Toole's valet and chauffeur in that memorable production of *Man and Superman*, and Estragon to Peter's Vladimir, during my National Service visits to the Bristol Old Vic. Donald McWhinnie directed.

Next came our first Shakespeare, *Twelfth Night*, with Dorothy Tutin repeating her Stratford success as Viola; Ian Holm as her twin, and Derek Godfrey and Geraldine McEwan as their eventual partners. A beautiful setting by Lila de Nobili. All this proved to be the 'warm-up' for our first world premiere, and our first commissioned script - *The Devils*, adapted from Aldous Huxley's book *The Devils of Loudun* by John Whiting: 'The story is elementarily simple' he said. 'A rakish and libertine priest of great character, high intelligence – well he wasn't, really, but I've made him so – has his women, his power. He is handsome, reasonably rich, and up at the convent is this lunatic Mother who suddenly has terrible ideas that Beelzebub is lodged in her stomach, and is speaking with the voice of the priest.

Local superstition, politics, fear, and revenge all allow people to come to believe it, and he is arrested, tried and burned. That's all: it could be put down on half a page'. The play – rather more than half a page - was directed by Peter Wood, with settings by Sean Kenny fresh from his triumph with the designs for Lionel Bart's *Oliver!* Dorothy Tutin and Richard Johnson headed the huge cast, with Diana Rigg 'plucked from the chorus' to take over as

Phillipe Trincant two weeks prior to the opening.

T C Worsley in The Guardian: 'I don't recall in twenty years of reviewing plays ever before having been tempted to use the word masterpiece about a new English play. But about Mr Whiting's *The Devils*, I am so tempted; and I shall not resist the temptation. The play demands as large a cast as any Shakespearean production and receives a first-class performance, fully justifying the whole of Mr Hall's venture'.

It was in 1961 that I got my first Lighting credits: two Sunday night presentations on the Aldwych stage. The first was 'an Entertainment by and about the Kings and Queens of England' put together by John Barton, under the title *The Hollow Crown*. It has since been seen almost everywhere, featuring many different members of the RSC (Peggy Ashcroft won the best actress award when part of the cast at the Theatre des Nations in Paris) and in 1963 the presentation played for six weeks in New York – all sadly without me. The second was a production of Strindberg's *Dance of Death* intended to give some of the junior members of the company a chance to perform principal roles, and staged without scenery - offering dramatic opportunities for the fledgling lighting designer which were noted by critic Eric Shorter in the Daily Telegraph: my first newspaper review.

By that time we had a second Shakespeare play in the repertoire: *The Taming of the Shrew*, a joyous revival of the previous year's Stratford production when Peter O'Toole and Peggy Ashcroft had been the principals. Derek Godfrey and Vanessa Redgrave replaced them at the Aldwych, so I missed out on my first opportunity to work with Peter; there will be another although not just yet: I do promise you, however, that the experience will be well worth the wait.

My first visit to Paris (there have been many since) was in 1963 when the Royal Shakespeare Company took Peter Brook's production of *King Lear* to the Festival des Nations at the Sarah Bernhardt Theatre. Paul Scofield was an old (but

not ancient) Lear; Irene Worth, Patience Collier and Diana Rigg the three daughters, with Alec McCowen as the Fool. That was my first experience of a 9.00pm curtain up, on a performance that didn't finish until well after midnight when Marlene Dietrich climbed onto her seat to lead a tremendous standing ovation. Even now I can remember how surprised and delighted we were to find the bars and cafes still open when we left the theatre.

The production had joined our Aldwych repertoire in November 1962 after playing for a week in Stratford to universally excellent reviews. *The Observer* critic, Kenneth Tynan, admitted that it was such an incomparable production that he could not pretend to the tranquillity in which emotion should properly be recollected, and preferred to quote from notes scrawled in the dark:-
'Flat white setting, combining Brecht and Oriental theatre. Everyone clad in luminous leather. Paul Scofield enters with grey crew-cut and peering gait, and with an old man's trick of dwelling on unexpected vowels. Brook means us to condemn his stupidity, and to respect the Fool who repeatedly tries to din his message into the deaf royal ears.

Top marks for Lear's drained, unsentimental reading of the lines about 'unaccommodated man': by now he is a rustic vagabond, a classless Samuel Becket derelict. The blinding of Gloucester could hardly be more shocking. And then, suddenly, greatness: Scofield's halting, apologetic delivery of 'I fear I am not in my right mind' and a Stoic determination, long in the moulding, to endure his going hence. Lighting deliberately bright throughout even during the nocturnal scenes, as in the Chinese theatre; and no music except towards the end when the text demands it. This production brings me closer to Lear than I have ever been'.

And Harold Hobson in *The Sunday Times*: 'The dark and terrible import of Mr Brook's production, intensified by the limitation of its scale, is that man is being watched, and that his presumption will not be forgiven. The meek shall inherit the earth only if an earth is left them to inherit' he added; a chilling thought which this meek author shares daily with the meek whales and the meek elephants and the meek rain forests.

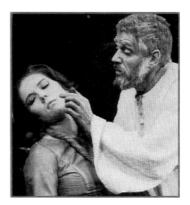

Would that an international tour of *King Lear* could solve the problems caused by man's presumption, arrogance and selfishness.

CHAPTER THIRTEEN
INTO THE WOODS - AT VINCENNES

For a few months in 1982 I was temporarily in charge of the British branch of the International Theatre Institute while the director was undergoing surgery. This involved a Paris meeting with officers of the French branch of the ITI, who invited me to join them at the first night of *Die Fledermaus* in the old Opera House.

Die Fledermaus proved to be one of the most bizarre productions I have ever seen, with bare-buttocked black dancers, and lighting which shone directly into our faces making it difficult to see the stage. The audience complained loudly throughout the performance, and roundly booed the director when he bravely, if foolishly, took a bow at the end.

La Cartoucherie, home of Théâtre du Soleil

At the suggestion of my French colleagues I made my first trip out to the Bois de Vincennes, to the Cartoucherie, home of the Théâtre du Soleil and their legendary director Ariane Mnouchkine – one of the first women to achieve an international reputation in this largely male-dominated profession: in my time only Joan Littlewood could claim comparative renown.

Théâtre du Soleil provided me with another unforgettable Paris evening, but this time for all the right reasons. The play was *Richard II*, and I still remember the sense of excitement, the outpouring of energy, the cut and colour of the costumes, the thrilling music, the dynamism of the movements. And, above all, the involvement gained by 'sharing the space' with the performers. It was like being back in the Mermaid at Puddle Dock except that this was not one warehouse, but three, and while watching the brilliantly directed and choreographed production in the central section, we were always aware of performers and props being made ready in the *wings*.

Despite the success of their previous show, *Mephisto*, the company was in debt. The new Socialist Minister of Culture Jack Lang doubled their grant, revived flagging spirits, and allowed them to 'raise the bar'. At a time when contemporary Shakespeare productions were being presented in a basically natural manner, Mnouchkine deliberately reversed the trend in order, she said, to emphasise the formality, the stylisation and the artificiality of Shakespeare's language and dramatic structure. They planned a season of three Shakespearean plays: *Richard II, Henry IV, part one,* and *Twelfth Night,* all to be performed in Oriental style. A backwards step, I thought, akin to Irving's declamatory Lyceum style returning to replace Poel's simplicity, although the Cartoucherie is an extremely large empty space and perhaps demands spectacle.

'And why Oriental?'
'Naturalism has to be avoided: do you think that when Henry IV appeared in public ceremonies he walked like everyone else? We wanted to escape from a realistic interpretation – tankards of beer, smoked ham and ruffians – which destroys all the poetry. Shakespeare's plays are much too big to be played psychologically. Oriental stylisation allowed us to depict a world which is not that of the everyday, but one full of magic and divinity'.

The financial crisis after *Mephisto* led to the departure of several original company members, some of whom had been colleagues of Ariane even before the formation of Théâtre du Soleil. The new, younger intake more readily accepted Ariane's leadership role: one of them, George Bigot, was cast as Richard II.

Following on from Copeau and Peter Brook, Mnouchkine used the concept of the empty space 'but that doesn't mean it has to be lugubrious or austere. I like purity but I hate austerity. I think the actor deserves a *magnificent* empty space'.

So the rough masonry walls of the performance area were painted gold, and at the back of the stage hung a succession of eleven enormous silk backcloths in red, grey, gold and silver. These were abstract, but reminiscent of suns and moons: they fell or were pulled down by the actors during the course of the performance, revealing the one behind it: a quick, simple, *incredibly-theatrical* scene change – much faster than Irving's twenty minutes.

Richard II had musicians – an Oriental band rather than an orchestra. They sat at one side of the stage and, in my memory, played almost continuously throughout: mainly percussion – muffled during dialogue but almost deafening during entrances and exits and action sequences. A gong accented key lines or moments. Text was declaimed rhythmically and at high volume rather than just spoken, and often delivered directly out front to the audience. Scenes on horseback were done in the style of Peking Opera. The costumes were based on *kabuki* but adapted to allow for running, leaping and the high kicks of the highly-choreographed movements, with elements which draped and floated and streamed behind the actors as they moved.

'Our survival depends on putting into the theatre that which can only exist within the theatre" said Ariane Mnouchkine, and survival was assured for a few more years by a sold-out production and the 1982 Grand Prix du Théâtre.

In their production *1789*, a version of the French Revolution as seen from the point of view of the ordinary people, they rewrote the history of the French Revolution in the light of the 1968 *événements*, the period of strikes, and civil disruption which had come close  to toppling the government. Members of the company had actually taken part in the protests. Rehearsals for *1789* included research (lectures and films on historical events); researching historical accounts; group improvisations on themes which came out of this research. 'All forms of theatre were attempted: direct address, *tableaux vivants*, opera, allegories, parliamentary debates. All events are covered, from the most inconsequential to the most significant. Thanks to the chosen form, even the most abstract subjects find a simple, direct and effective explanation. Every member contributes to this construction'.

 Ariane Mnouchkine explained how it all came together in an interview with theatre researcher Denis Bablet: 'In the production *1789* the company first expressed their ideas working in small groups, aiming for the most romantic, the most mythological of themes. The only early decision was how and where it should take place; this would be *in a fairground*, and acted by *bateleurs* (street performers)'.

Roberto Moscoco's set was developed from ideas for an abandoned production of Brecht's *Baal*.

How to follow a big success is always a problem: *1789*, and its *more reflective and philosophical sequel 1793* were successful, but led to a public demand for 'something closer to the present day social reality'. The successor production became *L'Age d'Or*: a contemporary story given necessary distance by imagining that the story is being told at some time in the future.

Respected commentators felt that *L'Age d'Or* confirmed the Théâtre du Soleil as the standard bearers for popular theatre: '*Since the end of Vilar's TNP, only one theatre company in France renews our reflection on the relationship between theatre and life, the insertion of theatre into the community and its chances of modifying the order of things in some way. It is the Théâtre du Soleil, led by Ariane Mnouchkine*'.

I was over in Paris researching this chapter during another typically-Parisian period of street protest, the *Gilets Jaunes* 'Ariane Mnouchkine has retired' I was told: 'her company is being directed by a Canadian, Robert Lepage (*below*). She won't be there'. I went out to La Cartoucherie to see his *Kanata* (Canada): part one, and found Ariane tearing tickets at the door. She was on a sabbatical to prepare her next production, she said, but 'couldn't stay away'. His production, *Kanata (part one)* was impressive but felt, I thought, like a television film somewhat clunkingly adapted for the stage: the scene changes were ingeniously and efficiently managed, but rather slowed down the action.

 We should briefly mention another Paris company doing similar work to Théâtre du Soleil, and led until recently by English director, Peter Brook. For forty years or more there was mutual admiration between his government-funded company at the Bouffes du Nord and the Théâtre du Soleil. Both directors, Brook and Mnouchkine, were influenced by Artaud and his Theatre of Cruelty; both were informed by Jan Kott's 1964 book *Shakespeare Our Contemporary* in which he drew a direct link between the Bard of Stratford on Avon and the modern European dramas of Brecht, Beckett and Durrenmatt. Can it be co-incidence that both Mnouchkine and Brook did memorable (and occasionally cruel?) productions of *A Midsummer Night's Dream*?

CHAPTER FOURTEEN
FROM THEATRE WORKSHOP
TO THEATRE OF CRUELTY

Peter Brook had been one of Peter Hall's co-Directors at the Royal Shakespeare Company, but only directed two productions during my time with them: *King Lear* was one, of course, and the other was James Kirkup's translation of Durrenmatt's *The Physicists*. Peter later 'collaborated' with Clifford Williams on a 1963 Stratford production of *The Tempest* with Tom Fleming as Prospero. One review called it *ill-conceived*: I can't comment because by then, I had been transferred to Joan Littlewood's Theatre Workshop at Stratford East.

Brook's view of Joan was 'some-one of tremendous talent, fired with a feeling which made her  little band of people – and all the work that went on in her theatre – as revolutionary, as dynamic and as exciting as any other aspect of those times'. He thought Joan's greatest asset was her ability to draw people out, to give them confidence and build them up. 'The thing an actor needs most is courage. The courage to get down to the footlights and do something silly, something which will make him look ridiculous. If an actor has enough guts and confidence to do this, then he's capable of doing wonderful things'.

 I remember one example of this: Joan was casting for a second *Oh What A Lovely War* company to tour in Britain and West Germany while the original cast was on Broadway. I discovered Nigel Hawthorne in the wings, the same Nigel Hawthorne who would later star as mad King George III.

This man who would go on to win major awards, and receive a knighthood, was practising silly walks. 'I swore I wouldn't do this' he said, 'but she gets to you, and you find that you want to give her the best silly walk you've ever done'. He did.

Stanislavsky provided the basis for much of Joan's work, but her application of his theory was no slavish adherence to a set of iron principles. She assimilated whatever was good and useful. Her other great influences were Rudolf Laban, who was fascinated by the undeveloped potential for movement and dance in the human body, and (as with Mnouchkine in Paris) the Italian *commedia dell'arte*.

The extraordinary series of productions of Elizabethan plays between 1954 and 1956 – *Volpone, Arden of Faversham, Richard II, Edward II* – were noted for their remarkable textual clarity, described as *like watching Shakespeare in one continuous shaft of lightning*. The stark simplicity of John Bury's sets and the perfectly disciplined group-playing of the company provided shows which were as fresh, exciting and meaningful as if they just been written. All Joan's work with actors had in mind, and relied on, that elusive thing (the precondition for the emergence of theatre art?) a permanent company. Her best work was when she managed to retain the same company over a long period.

A personal view from actress Vanessa Redgrave:
'I was a real old-fashioned girl: I loved red curtains, the razzmatazz, the trumpets, and the kings and queens. When my father (the actor Sir Michael Redgrave) sent me to see a 1954 Joan Littlewood production of *Richard II* at Stratford East I hated it. I automatically compared it to my father's production (two years previously at Stratford on Avon) and I was horrified by the fact that there was no scenery; there was no velvet, no colour, no pageantry. When my father asked 'What did you think?' I spieled off how much I'd hated it, and he got more and more solemn and began to look deadly disappointed. I realised something was terribly wrong, and he said 'I never, never want to hear you talk like that again.

When you go and see anything, you must first try to understand what they are trying to do, and why they are trying to do it. And when you've understood that, then you can say to yourself 'have they succeeded?' If you just ram out your own prejudices and preferences, you will understand nothing in the theatre, nothing in life'.

My father sent me to watch Joan rehearse, and that was fantastic, wonderful. Thrilling. I watched for a whole month, how she'd improvise and how she'd slam in a very friendly way, in a way that obviously everybody was totally used to, being very free and straightforward with each other. They were rehearsing a modern dress *Volpone*; Mosca gets thrown into the Grand Canal in Venice, so he went along the orchestra pit with a snorkel in his mouth. It was full of all kinds of invention. I was crazy about Joan Littlewood after that, and didn't want to see any of the other old kind of theatre'.

Joan's notes to the company following a performance of a long-running play: 'Can we stop regarding the audience as morons, cut out the rubbish, get back a bit of tension, pace and atmosphere? Can we stop wriggling our anatomies all over the script, over-acting, bullying laughs out of the audience, and playing for approbation? This hunger for approbation, which looks like selfishness, is mere insecurity and lack of trust in yourselves and each other.

You *cannot* play alone; stop wanting the audience to adore you and you only, they do anyway. People love actors and actresses, so relax – and let them have a look at the play for a change'.

One important element in Theatre Workshop's success was the *naturalistic illusion* of John Bury's designs for sets and lighting: he followed Craig's example and got rid of the footlights, and his sets included concrete walls and the original 'kitchen sink'. As I explained earlier, John had joined the new Royal Shakespeare Company to be their Head of Design at Stratford on Avon but had returned briefly to Stratford East to design and light *Oh What A Lovely War*.

Fully occupied with plans for the RSC *Wars of the Roses* season he was not available for *Lovely War*'s transfer into the West End. I was offered to Joan in 'part-exchange' and relit the production at Wyndham's Theatre - and again later for the British and German tours. Yes, they really did tour *Oh What a Lovely War* to West Germany, and with tremendous success: the Germans loved it. Sadly, John Bury made himself 'available' for the New York transfer so I missed out on my one and only chance to work on Broadway.

Theatre Workshop started in 1945 as a touring company in a hired lorry: they appeared regularly on the Edinburgh Fringe but eventually *life as a crowd of hungry bastards looking for somewhere to sell their talents* ceased to be fun.

Husband Ewan McColl left to become a folk singer. Joan and new partner/manager Gerry Raffles rented a dilapidated Theatre Royal in London's East End in 1953. Actors slept (illegally) in the dressing rooms while they refurbished the theatre and prepared their opening production, *Twelfth Night*. More classics followed: *Volpone, The Dutch Courtesan and Richard II*. A contemporary play, *The Good Soldier Schweik* (1955) was their first West End transfer. The company was regularly invited to the International Theatre Festival in Paris, and had eight further West End transfers, the greatest of which was *Oh What a Lovely War*. As I moved in, her company of *clowns* (her word) moved out to become stars in the West End – and later on Broadway. The focus of her fantastic energy was being dissipated.

I remained at Stratford East for a few months, lighting Joan's next production *Kayf Up West* (a Frank Norman play, with a young Barry Humphries in the cast), and some incoming touring shows, but things had changed. There was one later hit, *Mrs Wilson's Diaries,* after the *clowns'* return from America, but the fires were dying down. Her influence fortunately lives on in so many ways, and in so many memories: she was certainly a key part of my own personal learning curve and I recognise the *Littlewood touch* in many of my own scripts and productions.

Joan had a flat in Paris for many years and we met up there occasionally; her enthusiasm was ever infectious, and dinner in her favourite little Greek restaurant was a rewarding experience. On one occasion she 'reprised' her meeting that same afternoon with a couple of energetic and voluble American ladies, playing all three roles in an exhausting but brilliant *piéce du théâtre* which had the entire restaurant in stitches – a reminder, if we needed it, that she was also an extremely capable and experienced actress: indeed, she was the first in Britain to play Mother Courage. 30th June 1955 at the Queens Hall, Barnstaple as part of the Devon Arts Festival. The twelve-strong Theatre Workshop company had played *Richard II* for the first half of the week and *Mother Courage* was desperately under-rehearsed, but Harold Hobson still found it a *work of quality.*

Joan Littlewood was a wonderful, inspirational lady, whose achievements and talents were highly praised and feted abroad, but insufficiently acknowledged at home - although there was one occasion when they might have been: the Royal Shakespeare Company invited her to direct a production of Shakespeare's Henry IV. Arriving early for work one morning at the Aldwych I discovered her dodging the cleaners and 'getting the feel' of the auditorium and the stage. She had obviously decided to do a recce. She and John Bury did go to Stratford-on-Avon, but Joan later pulled out of the production and went off to Nigeria: probably the right decision: she would have hated the *Stratford West* bureaucracy, and hated even more the fact that her *clowns* would have spent more time on the road between Stratford and London, or appearing in other repertoire productions, than they did in the rehearsal room. John Bury stayed on, and – apart from *Oh What a Lovely War* - spent the rest of his career with the RSC and then the National Theatre.

When we eventually ran out of steam at Stratford East I freelanced for a while, returning to the RSC for occasional projects - usually to relight their touring productions but once to assist with a strange little season of *Theatre of Cruelty* at the LAMDA Theatre Club in early 1964 organised and directed by Peter Brook and Charles Marowitz.

In her *Concise History of The Theatre*, Phyllis Hartnoll explains that the Theatre of Cruelty derived from the work of Antonin Artaud (1896-1948) *(left) who was connected with the surrealist movement* and *died insane*.

Some readers may feel inclined to move to the next chapter at this point, but I'll plough on to see where it takes us. In his *History of Theatre in Europe* John Allen describes Artaud as 'a tortured Frenchman, one of the great visionaries'. His ideas were important to Peter Brook whose theatrical experiments revealed new concepts of theatrical art, sometimes of a non-linguistic nature, though hardly deserving the term *cruel*. His *concept* came into England with Brook's RSC production at the Aldwych Theatre in August 1964 of Peter Weiss's *Persecution and Assassination of Marat as Performed by the Inmates of the Asylum of Charenton under the Direction of the Marquis de Sade,* a work fortunately known more briefly as *The Marat/Sade*.

'The *Marat/Sade* was absolutely radical and avant-garde' says playwright David Hare. 'Rich text, great acting, physical performances. It changed British theatre for ever'.

The short 1964 *Theatre of Cruelty* season at LAMDA was intended as Mnouchkine-style workshops and performances in preparation for the forthcoming *Marat/Sade* production, and mostly involved newcomers to the company. One of these, Glenda Jackson, would go on to play the leading role of Charlotte Corday in *Marat/Sade* (and much else in both theatre and films) prior to a successful political career. None of the other principals in *The Marat/Sade* – Freddie Jones, Clive Revell, Ian Richardson, Clifford Rose, Elizabeth Spriggs and Timothy West – were involved in the *Theatre of Cruelty LAMDA* season and, as far as I can remember, none of them even attended its performances, so the season may have had little or no point.

Some believe that it was the quality of Peter Weiss's script for *The Marat/Sade* which ensured that production's success, rather than anything learnt during the LAMDA Studio sessions. Charles Marowitz claims that the season was never intended as a *show*, but merely a demonstration of work in progress; of interest, they assumed, to the profession. The press were not invited in the usual way, but were welcome: a self-delusion by Brook and Marowitz. Only after the event did they realise that any presentation performed before an audience, invited or otherwise, becomes a show.

A show which will be judged according to traditional criteria. 'We weren't really intending a theatrical performance', said Peter Brook: this same Peter Brook who, you will recall, wrote 'a man walks across an empty space while someone else is watching him, and this is all that is needed for an act of theatre to be engaged'.

Clive Barker attended, and 'thought the season was a dismal failure, both in terms of finding solutions to the problems posed, or keeping any sort of faith with the ideas propounded by Artaud, 'although I gained from the performances in the development of my own work and understood that the training of actors was a crucial issue to be addressed if the British theatre was to move forward'. After Brook moved to Paris, Clive Barker joined an audience of school-children there, witnessing Brook's *work in progress*: 'the experience was as enlightening and enlivening as the *Theatre of Cruelty* had been stultifying'.

Incidentally, the company definition of *Theatre of Cruelty* was 'paying the actors only £12 a week'.

John Allen also mentioned the influence of Artaud on the Polish director Jerzy Grotowski (1933-1999). Khalid Tyabji worked with the Second Studio of Wroclaw under Zbigniew Cynkutis and later translated his book *Acting with Grotowski* (Routledge, 2015). According to him Grotowski saw Artaud as 'the visionary poet of a new theatre that would transcend discursive reason and psychology.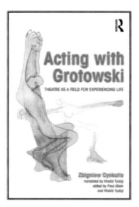
One could say that his entire theatre work was, in a way, devolved to discovering the magic that Artaud had envisioned, but for which he had provided few recipes'.

No recipes, perhaps, but Artaud did provide 'ingredients' in the form of a 1934 Manifesto:

We intend to do away with stage and auditorium, replacing them with a single, undivided locale without any partitions of any kind. The audience will be in the centre of the action, encircled by it, seated on swivel chairs allowing them to follow the action.

Our *Theatre of Cruelty* season certainly attempted this: the LAMDA Studio's steeply-raked semi-circular auditorium had the performance area spreading forward into the half-circle central space. The Directors decided to put the audience seating in the stage area, with the performers working on the steep steps of the auditorium 'semi-encircling' the audience.

We must discover oscillating light effects, new ways of diffusing lighting in waves, sheet lighting like a flight of fire arrows. Sensations of heat, cold, anger, fear and so on.

I was supposed to be lighting this season, but we never discussed any of the above, and the directors never thought to involve us, or to ask for any of these effects. It might have been fun to try. However, since the studio's lighting rig was mainly aimed towards the original stage, now the auditorium, getting any light at all onto the performers was already difficult; 'cruel', even.

Every show will contain physical, objective elements perceptible to all. Shouts, groans, apparitions, surprise, abrupt lighting changes, masks, puppets many feet high, rare musical notes, etc.

I don't remember too many puppets, of any height. I do remember some nudity, not mentioned in the Manifesto.

Theatre will never be itself again unless it provides the audience with truthful distillations of dreams where its taste for crime, its erotic obsessions, its fantasies, its savageness, its utopian sense of life and objects, even cannibalism, do not gush out on an illusory make-believe but on an inner level.

Ah, yes, I forgot the erotic obsessions and fantasies. Perhaps nudity was a 'truthful distillation of a dream'? Cannibalism was in short supply, but that was probably a good thing since we didn't have any understudies.

The old duality between author and director will disappear. This one is intriguing on several levels: as we have seen, the role of Director had only been around for about forty years and was generally accepted as an improvement on what had happened before. I remember attending a rather confusing lecture by playwright Peter Barnes when he suggested – I'm sure I got this right – that playwrights were the only people able to direct their own plays because only they knew the author's intentions. Carried to a logical conclusion this would mean that we could have only productions of plays by living playwrights, and there would be few new plays because the successful playwrights would be too busy chasing around the world directing productions of those existing plays. Sorry, Mr Barnes: that's nonsense. Tyrone Guthrie appeared to agree with me: 'It is not wise for authors to direct their own work. An interpreter with a fresh eye and ear, and without an author's over-tenderness towards his own brainchild, is a valuable intermediary between a script and its audience'.

J B Priestley considered that the French were far ahead of us in two respects: they had talented directors in control, and playwrights who understood where the director could help them. William Gaskill also supported the principle of 'duality' believing that directors should certainly liaise with playwrights over their intentions, although Jonathan Miller pointed out the difficulties of discovering the intentions of a dead author. George Devine felt that writers were 'talents who should be helped to find their own direction'.

I sometimes have to direct productions of my own scripts – usually for financial reasons - but am always aware that I am only directing what I know I have written: there may be things in those scripts that I don't know I've written, and which a different or better director might have discovered.

I also cannot direct what I don't know I haven't written; and this is another strong argument for the 'duality' of writer and director; witness an entry in Richard Eyre's *Diaries*: 'Good read-through of a draft of *The Absence of War*: felt very powerful, but there's a scene missing in the second half".

The 'duality' of Alan Bennett and Nicholas Hytner is a well-documented example: Alan's note accompanying the first draft of *The History Boys* said 'It's full of gaps and repetitions, plus lots of odd bits  which aren't fully worked out', and he admits to being surprised when Nick Hytner 'saw its potential and straightaway took it on. Nobody else would have known what to do with it, or helped me to shape it in the way he did - and with no disagreement or heartache'. There are more fascinating revelations about the working methods of this 'duality' in Nicholas Hytner's book *Balancing Acts*.

In Artaud's own book *The Theatre and its Double* he wrote 'No one has ever proved word language is the best' and hints at a 'sign language'; words effacing themselves behind gesture. I have some sympathy with the argument that drama in Britain often appears to depend more on the voice than the body: Tynan, I think, said the British act with their voices; foreigners with their lives. Harold Hobson wrote of 'Shaftesbury Avenue actors in their lounge suits treating the body as though *rigor mortis* had set in' and realising that *exuberance* was one of the lessons French theatre could teach us - especially the exuberance of Jean-Louis Barrault, the *greatest theatrical animateur of the age*.

Hobson had recently seen Barrault at the 1948 Edinburgh Festival, 'performing with every part of his body and not merely with the voice'.

Yet this same Artaud, who has doubts about the efficiency of *word language*, passes his thoughts down to us in a book. Words, words, words! My view, for what it's worth, is that it is the directing half of the duality who adds the 'sign language' and the stage picture, giving three-dimensional life to the playwright's words and thoughts - although always, always, remembering that it is the playwright's story.

Artaud's theories are said to have encouraged the savageries of David Rudkin's play *Afore Night Comes*, where a farm-labourer is decapitated and torn in pieces, and the stoning of a baby in its pram in Edward Bond's *Saved*. Surely cruelty was evident in our theatre long before the *tortured Frenchman* came along? The Greeks, for instance; *Titus Andronicus*, much of Marlowe, the final scene of *Madame Butterfly (*and many other operas). In our first RSC season at the Aldwych we tortured Father Grandier in *The Devils*: in the second season we put out Gloucester's eyes in *King Lear*: no one referenced Artaud.

CHAPTER FIFTEEN
PHILOSOPHY AND THE OUTSIDER

I suppose that the subject of this book - my search for a purpose, a destiny - makes some mention of philosophy inevitable, although until now it is not something I have ever seriously considered. When I was studying book-keeping at evening classes in the 1950s my then boss, Fulham's Borough Treasurer, suggested that I should also do a philosophy course. I lasted about three weeks. To a teenager, existentialism or whatever as a universal 'lifestyle' seemed wildly impractical: believing that the whole of mankind should go around acting as they each saw fit appeared to me a recipe for chaos on a grand scale.

Except, of course, it wouldn't be 'the whole of mankind'. Kierkegaard, the Danish philosopher wrote 'Life can only be understood backwards, but it must be lived forwards'. Existentialists believed that a person should be forced to choose, and to be responsible *without the help of laws, ethnic rules or traditions*. It seems to me that even without these (especially without these?) you must have considerable experience of life 'understood backwards' before you can make great decisions about potential onward 'forward living'. No five-year-old existentialists, then, and probably no teenage existentialists so I was wasting my time at evening classes when I could have been at drama rehearsals.

On the subject of 'choice' Sartre believed 'a person can choose to act in a different way; to be a good person instead of a cruel person' but philosophical definitions of good or bad, kind or cruel, right or wrong, are far from clear-cut - especially Nietzsche's whose definitions I frankly found incomprehensible. *Good* and (according to Nietzsche) *evil* were defined for my generation through weekly attendance at Sunday school, and by morning assembly – including hymn and prayer – at both junior and grammar schools. And, for a while, in the church choir at St Matthews: I can still sing *Non Nobis Domine* and *Zadok the Priest* from memory – although now on the bass line. Anthems for a doomed youth.

In my lifetime I have seen so much inhumanity carried out in the name of one god or another; so much death and destruction both to peoples and to the planet which is our shared and only home, that I see no proof of a god or of a heaven. Sometimes the opposite: hoping for better things in the hereafter might prevent us working harder to improve life in the present. However, that early education, basically Anglican, left me with the sense that a world operating according to the principles of the Ten Commandments might not be such a bad place. The Commandments are Old Testament, and therefore common to Jews, Muslims and Christians, though you wouldn't think so given the way they all carry on.

For Frank Field, a committed Anglican, 'the Christian story just seems to me to make more sense than any other'. Field, a politician and an outsider, told Lynn Barber 'I grew up a loner, and have remained a loner. I did most things alone, right from the early days, even at school or university. I could have had friends but, looking back, I can see that I did most things by myself'. An outsider who has obviously found *his tambourine*, he is now comfortable with his life: 'I love every day, and that is such a privilege, compared to people who work in a job they loathe'. Perhaps Nietzsche was right when he said '"He who has a *why* to live can bear almost any *how*'.

Nietzsche thought that exceptional people should no longer be ashamed of their uniqueness in the face of a supposed morality-for-all, and should follow their own *inner law* – suggesting, apparently, that *exceptional* people might be self-anointed? John Elsom has written that his study of existentialism allowed him to believe that 'he could become anything that he wanted to be' but presumably he is sufficiently sensible to put practical limits to his desires. No point in *wanting to be* immortal. Or, indeed, exceptional?

'To live is to suffer, to survive is to find some meaning in the suffering' was Nietzsche's view, but with so many philosophers, so many philosophies: how do you choose? 'One should choose a theatre as one chooses a temple' said George Devine, but to choose a philosophy with which you agree is the easy way out.

Surely one should seek a philosophy which offers the hope of a better, fairer world? For everyone, not just for ourselves. Something better than we have at present. As the song says, 'There's got to be something better than this' although what we seek will vary from person to person, family to family, business to business, government to government, country to country. And, inevitably, philosopher to philosopher. We are, each of us, all searching for *our own tambourine* and presumably hoping to recognise it when we find it. I found mine: the majority probably won't.

Especially in a world which is racing rapidly downhill: a digital world where a major nation can be governed entirely by tweets; where social media can openly dissipate false information, or the personal details of its users; where elections can be affected by international hackers; where dissidents can be poisoned, or killed and chopped up in a foreign country far from home. Whenever you are reading this, unless we can turn the tide, or *find some meaning in the suffering*, today may well be, not *your last day*, but possibly the *best day* of the rest of your life.

John Ezard, who died three years before Colin Wilson, had fortuitously already prepared Wilson's obituary for The Guardian. In it he wrote 'Wilson's book, *The Outsider*, remains extraordinary, more for its reach than its grasp'. Wilson looked for the path through case studies of the agonies and ecstasies of thinkers, artists and men of action.

His list included Friedrich Nietzsche, Jean-Paul Sartre, Albert Camus, Ernest Hemingway, Vaslav Nijinsky, Vincent van Gogh, Hermann Hesse and Lawrence of Arabia. He condensed them into a single type, 'the Outsider, a questing spirit straddled between devastating experiences of nothingness and moments of the highest insight'.

Colin Wilson introduced William Blake as 'very definitely a *religious Outsider*' and it was at this point I began seriously questioning his arguments: surely his chosen *thinkers, artists and men of action* are not examples of a *type* but essentially *individuals*, outside society, unique in themselves, in their *outsidedness*. There is no *community* of outsiders posing beneath a multi-coloured flag. There aren't any support groups, or drop-in centres, or appeals for understanding and tolerance, or campaigns for equal rights for outsiders. They are what they are or, as the Outsider would put it, 'I am what I am' (another song title).

Wilson's *Outsider* was published by Victor Gollancz in May 1956, the same month as the premiere of John Osborne's play *Look Back in Anger* at the Royal Court. Wilson and Osborne were the first of the 'angry young men' hyped, and then harassed, by the press. Ezard concluded 'Colin Wilson was Britain's first, and so far last, home-grown existentialist star, but his philosophy and religion ceased to be seen as mainstream topics after the 1950s'.

Stoppard's play *Travesties* remembers James Joyce as 'a complex personality, a contradictory spokesman for the truth, an enigma, an obsessive litigant and yet an essentially private man who wished his total indifference to public notice to be universally recognised'. This *desire to be recognised* is echoed by Alan Bennett's wonderful *Beyond The Fringe* description of T E Lawrence: 'Clad in the magnificent white silk robes of an Arab prince with, in his belt, the short curved, gold sword of the  Ashraf descendants of the Prophet, he hopes to pass unnoticed through London', reminding me of Henry Miller's belief 'It is not love of the self but dread of the world outside the self which is the seed of narcissism'.

Wilson grouped together three *examples* - van Gogh, Lawrence and Nijinsky – having in common, he suggests, one unfortunate feature: 'they all believed that they had nothing, and that they deserved nothing. They did not understand themselves, and consequently wasted their powers'. Wilson 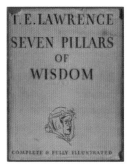 considered *Seven Pillars of Wisdom* 'one of the most important case-books of the Outsider that we possess'. T E Lawrence sent an early linotype copy of his *awkward and prodigious work* to G B Shaw; 'I may profit by your reading it'. Shaw and his wife Charlotte both read it and 'left not a paragraph without improvement'.

Shaw advised him on his contract with the publishers, Jonathan Cape. Charlotte read the proofs of the book. 'One of the great books of the world' GBS told Lady Gregory, who recorded that 'the two people most on Shaw's mind at that time were Joan of Arc and Lawrence of Arabia', both unconventional military leaders brought down by politicians. 'Lawrence is not normal in many ways', D G Hogarth advised Shaw, 'and it is extraordinarily difficult to do anything for him'. 'I am rather a difficult person to help' Lawrence himself admitted. Shaw and Charlotte bought him the motor cycle on which he was killed.

Interestingly, Colin Wilson's role model from the age of 13 was G B Shaw: he actually wrote about him in *Bernard Shaw: A Reassessment (1969)*. *Lacking the conceit of other men of genius* was identified by Wilson as a major handicap in any Outsider's search for his *own tambourine*, but I wonder if Wilson is correct in believing that *they didn't understand themselves*. I suspect that some, at least, of his example Outsiders understood themselves only too well. Their problem was that they didn't *like* themselves – a much stronger reason, surely, for *lacking conceit*. 'I did not like the *myself* that I could see and hear' wrote Lawrence in *Seven Pillars*. Robert Graves, seeing Orpen's portrait of Lawrence, remarked on 'a sort of street-urchin furtiveness'.

In *Steppenwolf* Hesse writes of his *anti-hero* 'His whole life was an example that love of one's neighbour is not possible without love of oneself; that self-hate is really the same thing as sheer egoism and in the long run breeds the same cruel isolation and despair', although I appreciate that by quoting a fictional character to illustrate a *real-life social problem* I am now copying Colin Wilson's error when he made similar use of Camus' fictitious *outsider* Meursault.

So much for philosophy.

CHAPTER SIXTEEN
TOWARDS A NATIONAL THEATRE

In an 1877 pamphlet, William Archer and R W Lowe criticised the mannerisms of Henry Irving and pointed to a need for a permanent school of acting in England: 'the only remedy lies in a national theatre with good endowment, good traditions and good government. So long as actors have to trust for their training to their own haphazard requirements; so long as the only one condition of their very existence is that they should please a tasteless gallery and even more tasteless stalls; so long as every artistic instinct in their nature is liable to be ruined by a two hundred nights' run; so long will histrionic talent, especially of the loftier orders, be unavoidably doomed to the same destiny which has destroyed the unquestionable gifts of Mr Henry Irving'.

As early as 1873 Archer had been asking 'When shall we in England have a National Theatre?' In 1900 Archer and Granville-Barker led a committee, prepared a scheme, and received approval of leading actors, but the money could not be found. With Shaw's help they prepared a manifesto, drew up budgets, even laid a foundation stone, but to no avail. There were serious doubters about both the need and the style of any new organisation. For years it had been assumed that a 'national theatre company' might follow on naturally from the work being done at the Old Vic. Max Beerbohm was a doubter: 'However elastic the intentions of its pious founder, a National Theatre would inevitably, sooner or later – and, I think, sooner – sink into majestic academism, and be nothing but a great rich paddock for the war-horses of the past'.

In 1962 plans were drawn up for a major three-auditoria construction on the South Bank to become the future home of the new National Theatre Company being put together by the most obvious choice as Director, Sir Laurence Olivier. He selected as his assistants two of George Devine's team at the Royal Court, John Dexter and William Gaskill.

They may possibly have been recommended by Lady Olivier, the actress Joan Plowright, the first Royal Court 'star' created under Devine's regime - although Olivier himself, of course, had Royal Court 'form' having starred there in 1957 as *The Entertainer* in John Osborne's musical play, and co-starred with Joan Plowright in Orson Welles production of *The Rhinoceros*.

Of his 'job interview' William Gaskill wrote: 'What Olivier called *the wooing of Billy Gaskill* was done mostly over lunches at the Dorchester. Of course I succumbed: who wouldn't have? The idea of an ensemble haunted all our dreams: long-term contracts, adequate rehearsal time, and the development of new methods of acting, direction and design would be possible. All this had previously only happened in Europe: now I would have a chance to put some of my ideas into practice'. Olivier and his two assistants gathered together a widely-experienced and talented company who would – apart from a couple of summers at Chichester - perform at the Old Vic until the new National Theatre complex was ready for them. The programme for their first Old Vic season would consist of two Shakespeares, an Ibsen, a Chekhov, a Restoration Comedy (*The Recruiting Officer*, directed by Gaskill), a Greek Tragedy, a play of the Manchester School (*Hobson's Choice*, directed by John Dexter) and – joining *the war-horses of the past in the paddock* - two new plays.

My own *wooing* took place on the lawns behind Chichester's Festival Theatre. I had received a phone message: Olivier want to see you – ask for him at the stage door. He came out in his shirtsleeves, and we sat and chatted on the grass. He explained that during that first season at the Old Vic he had used guest designers for both sets and lighting: naturally they all wanted to create a good impression and made such full use of the facilities (and budgets) that the theatre staff were finding it difficult to change the scenery and refocus/recolour practically every lantern in the building in the short time between end of rehearsals and curtain up - plus, twice a week, between matinee and evening performance.

'What I want you to do' he said 'is to join us as resident lighting designer for the second season, and design a basic lighting rig which will adapt quickly to the different productions'. Inexperienced as I was, I knew that this was an impossible dream: at that stage only the early productions were scheduled and yet I was supposed to plan a permanent rig to suit shows which were as yet not even designed. So why did I agree? Stupid question; even knowing that I was on a hiding to nothing I wasn't about to turn down a year at the National Theatre with Olivier and Franco Zeffirelli and Noel Coward and the cream of British acting talent. And it would only be a year: the designers would continue to fill the stage with happy scenery whilst I was denied the opportunity to light the shows properly. The imbalance would become increasingly obvious as the season progressed, and the experiment would not be repeated.

If it was an unhappy year for me, it was a wonderful year for the company. We churned out new productions and revivals every three weeks or so, to a generally high standard and to a generally supportive press and audience. The atmosphere engendered by Olivier was superb: the intimacy of the Old Vic could have been limiting but actually produced a genuine 'company feeling', all in it together as Jonathan Miller remembered: 'In the 1960s when the National Theatre was in its comparatively modest setting at the Old Vic it had a sort of sloppy, raffish charm, and was still run by someone, Laurence Olivier, who had both a practical, knockabout working relationship with the stage and was familiar with everyone'. That 'familiarity' was the key to the early success of this 'slim-line' company. He knew everyone – including the Old Vic staff – and we all respected and adored him. That closeness was unlikely to transfer to the wide open spaces of the South Bank'. It didn't, of course, as Denis Quilley remembered: 'In a place the size of the South Bank you can't have that same kind of communal feeling. The circumstances are so different, it's not the same family situation. You can't do what Larry did, training up people like Tony Hopkins and Ronnie Pickup from spear-carriers to stars'.

During my year at the Old Vic we had a couple of *guest* directors: Noel Coward directing his own play *Hay Fever*, and Franco Zeffirelli with an irreverent production of *Much Ado About Nothing*. In amongst a great deal of 'carping' the Times critic enjoyed *Much Ado*: 'A nattily uniformed town band parades the streets blaring forth crudely-harmonised marches (playing music commissioned from Nino Rota, recipient of an Oscar for his Godfather scores): the troops swagger back from the war in dress swords and plumed pill-box hats and are mobbed by a welcoming crowd of frock-coated civilians. The sweating sun-blown splendour and squalor lent Claudio's accusation credibility.

Pamela Mason's was another positive voice: 'The human statues moving and freezing on stage contributed to a carnival atmosphere. Even Derek Jacobi's Don John was comic – petulant, neurotic and hyperactive. Dogberry had a thick Italian accent and Verges rode a bicycle. The successful church scene began comically, which made Claudio's rejection intensely shocking. The savage force of Beatrice's 'Kill Claudio!' stunned both the audience and Benedick, whose reply 'not for the wide world' was whispered.

And it all ended in *a moment of magic* as Albert Finney's strutting, Spanish-accented Don Pedro controlled the closing moments, looking up at the single lamp illuminating the stage, and bowing just as the final note of music plunged everything into darkness'.

Zeffirelli's own reaction to the *furore* was suitably modest: 'Olivier and I did one of the most wonderful productions ever seen; *Much Ado About Nothing*, a truly memorable Shakespearian play with a cast of great actors who enjoyed themselves like mad. I managed to stir up general madness where everyone was happy to be there from the youngest to the oldest: from Maggie Smith to Albert Finney, from Robert Stephens to Frank Finlay; just about everyone was there. They had a wonderful time and I enjoyed making them have fun. And the audience in turn enjoyed itself: it really was a lot of fun'.

I don't remember much fun with our production of *Mother Courage*. In *Subsequent Performances* Jonathan Miller wrote 'the inflexible determination to preserve a play in the image of the first production can sometimes do the author a terrible disservice, and the play can become mummified by dogma'. He instanced Chekhov, whose widow *supervised the proprieties to the smallest detail* with the result that the orthodox productions began to look quaint, and even irrelevant. *Something comparable,* he thought, *happened to Wagner and Brecht.*

It certainly happened to Brecht in our production: I got on well with Bill Gaskill (he even sounded me out about moving with him to the Royal Court) but he was dedicated to the 'model books' which recorded all of the Berliner Ensemble productions. Bill believed that Brecht's original production of *Mother Courage* was *perfection* and set out to copy it as closely as possible, *preserving it in aspic* to quote Richard Eyre, rather than finding a formula to encompass the wider talents and experience of a widely talented and experienced company (several of whom – Robert Stephens, Frank Finlay and Colin Blakely, for instance – had actually been recruited from the Royal Court).

Dame Edith Evans joined the company to play Judith Bliss in Noel Coward's *Hay Fever*, directed by the author himself. The great lady was by then in her late seventies, still with

tremendous ability and star quality, but nervous about playing someone twenty years younger and, on the first night, not at all confident about her lines. There was one small hiatus requiring several loud prompts, and one sensed the tension both on stage and in the audience. Happily, a few minutes later, she pitched one of Coward's wittier lines absolutely perfectly and got a huge laugh. Everyone relaxed, and the evening was a great success. If I have one regret about my *career* it's that it started just too late to catch that generation of actors at their peak, doing what they did best, playing Shakespeare at Stratford and the Old Vic. They had an aura, didn't they? – perhaps because they weren't continually in our homes in magazine interviews or radio quizzes or taking part in 'reality' television shows.

I recall James Agate on Sarah Bernhardt: 'When, after her performance of Pelleas in Maeterlinck's play at the Theatre Royal, Manchester, Sarah Bernhardt walked through the winter garden of the Midland Hotel, hard-headed cotton

manufacturers who had never heard of her stood up and removed their bowler hats, and common stockbrokers, abashed and open-mouthed, left their stories in the air'.

Happily, I was around to light Olivier's Othello, reviewed here by Robert Speaight:
'Until yesterday, Othello, the Everest among Shakespearian parts, had been scaled only by Edmund Kean. Sir Laurence Olivier's triumph was always predictable: I never doubted that he would electrify but I was less certain that he would convince.

Taking a hint from Dr Leavis, he presents an Othello of noble but self-deluding egotism, the seeds of whose undoing are within. The tragic grandeur of the part is in no way impaired by this conception; only Iago is reduced by it, but Mr Frank Finlay unselfishly serves the grand design. I found Sir Laurence's speaking of the Shakespearean verse – or, better, his acting of it – personal without being in the least perverse.

The words are chiselled as they spring, new minted, from his mind and heart. None of the great things are lost, or even blurred: the pace is deliberate, but never drags; and every pause has meaning. Some of these are inspired, as when Othello, in the first throes of jealousy, stumbles before the word 'love' – matching the pathos of 'Cassio hath my place' and 'O the pity of it' when he effaces himself against the wall.

The earlier scenes have a leisurely and even humorous self-confidence, and the sensuality, though evident, is never over-stressed. For all its realism Olivier's Othello has a refinement, a kind of spiritual lightness, a romantic gallantry: this is great acting indeed. Miss Smith's Desdemona comes into its own during the later scenes.

Mr Dexter's production is inventive without fussiness. Miss Jocelyn Herbert's décor has sombre spaciousness'. That 'spaciousness' allowed me to sneak in rather more atmospheric lighting than had been possible on other productions, but the principals proved difficult: Olivier had a dark black make-up and black costume, while Maggie Smith's Desdemona was in a startlingly-white night-dress. I used a lot of blue light which toned down the whiteness of the dress, and seemed to reflect better from the black pancake, and was intrigued to see that Stuart Burge adopted something similar in his later film of the production.

My year ended with *The Crucible*, directed by Olivier, and with its author Arthur Miller in the first-night audience. Designer was Michael Annals (known in the production offices as Tiny Alice - I didn't ask why). I liked his sets (Bill Gaskill didn't) although the huge roof timbers hanging above the stage did me no favours with the lighting. That was the final production before the company decamped to Chichester for the summer. I took my leave of Sir Laurence with a certain amount of mutual regret: I because I was fully aware that our system had limited the artistic potential of most of the productions, and he because that failure would mean a return to the delayed curtain-ups while the staff struggled to complete both stage and lighting re-sets in the limited time (and extremely limited space) available when they returned from Chichester in the autumn.

Olivier thought I was off to Bayreuth to stage manage Wagner Opera. In fact, I was off to Beirut to stage manage topless cabaret in a Las Vegas-style Casino and Night Club but, still in awe of the great man, I didn't correct him.

By the time the new South Bank building was ready Olivier had reluctantly handed on responsibility to his appointed successor. He was exhausted by a debilitating illness, by censorship problems over the planned production of Hochhuth's play *Soldiers*, and by a volatile relationship with his 'dramaturg' Ken Tynan. 'I had always dreamed of marching my little troupe up the road but the South Bank wasn't for me' Olivier wrote: 'I was hoping to feel a glow of satisfaction but I was so tired out, I was just glad to let it go'. Olivier had described the job as 'the most tiresome, awkward, embarrassing, forever-compromising, thankless post that anyone could be fool enough to take on'. His successor fool was, almost inevitably, Peter Hall.

There was a considerable amount of what can only be described as *bitchiness* about the new regime, mainly from the purple-suited *dramaturg*, Ken Tynan.

2.5.74: First play at the Old Vic under Peter Hall regime: *Next of Kin* by John Hopkins; directed by Harold Pinter. *A bleak and monotonous exposé of suburbia*. It would be madness to go to a Peter Hall presentation in the expectation of being moved to tears either of laughter of grief. You will get clarity, tact, restraint, lucid exposition – all the Cambridge virtues – but you will not be made to *feel*: that vulgar weapon is not in Peter Hall's armoury.

'I note with some pleasure that Michael Billington in today's Guardian expresses serious doubts about the current direction of policy at the NT. I really think that Larry and I presided over a golden age (there's *modesty!*). Granted we started with one let-down (*Hamlet*) but Peter Hall has started with three'.

25.1.75: To the Old Vic for a preview of Peter Hall's production of *John Gabriel Borkman*, with the sort of cast that Binkie Beaumont would have given it fifteen years ago (Ralph Richardson, Peggy Ashcroft, Wendy Hiller). Hall has now had a year at the helm and one has a frantic sense of a ship that has run hopelessly aground: a few oars swing furiously in their rowlocks, beating at air, and there's no breeze around to fill the sails.

Why *this* Ibsen, anyway? It's like a Pinter play dressed up in frock-coats and bombazine. The last act – with Borkman and Ella out in the snow – was frankly hilarious. What a mess Peter Hall has made of *our* theatre!

29.1.75: Appalled to read three glowing reviews of the NT's *John Gabriel Borkman*.

9.2.75: Joan Plowright (Lady Olivier) joins in the joshing: 'Hall and John Barton once watched a Stratford dress rehearsal of *Two Gentlemen of Verona*, directed by Robin Phillips, and were appalled; so much so that there was talk of cancellation. The preview audience was rapturous so they summoned Phillips for 'a chat'. 'What was your concept in this production?' asked Hall. Philips looked puzzled. 'What was your governing idea?' asked Barton. 'I didn't have one' said Philips, 'It just happened between me and the actors'.

They couldn't understand how anyone could stage a play without first writing a 1000-word programme note 'reinterpreting the play for contemporary audiences'.

10.2.75: NT Board 'shaken to the core' by the Hall regime, not least by the appalling cost of it all: in addition to his own vast salary and perks (including a flat in the Barbican and a chauffeur-driven car) he employs two assistants to whom he delegates authority, over the heads of the associate directors, and now we must add to all that his astonishing decision to take over the TV arts programme *Aquarius* – an act of bizarre effrontery with the NT in such a fragile condition. A decision taken in the face of unanimous opposition from his associate directors'. Hall later added operatic commitments in Glyndebourne and Bayreuth, and visits to Broadway with National Theatre transfers.

Tynan again: 12.9.75: Over lunch Larry chats unhappily about the National, lamenting that under the Hall regime all sense of company solidarity has gone. 'It isn't a company any more. They just cast each production from scratch out of Spotlight: that wasn't what this National Theatre was created for. That wasn't what we fought for all those years'. 'Larry's contract with the NT expires next month. He is frailer than I remember him, and has difficulty climbing the stairs. He will never appear on the stage again, although he has several big film parts lined up'.

 As Jonathan Miller, saw it 'the National Theatre became a great complex on the South Bank encouraging an episcopal largeness of style reflecting the view of the management (and those performers invited by the management) that what they were doing was too important to be performed in a slipshod, casual way. As Olivier's liberating raffishness disappeared the organisation began to die. Under the executive ambition of Peter Hall the National Theatre became an institution that was too grandly self-important. Theatre is best when it maintains spontaneity.

From Peter Hall's Diary (after the opening night of *Macbeth*): The notices are as terrible as any I have had. After five minutes of blind anger I settled down and got on with the job. It's the only way.

Hall's successor, Richard Eyre: 'Peter had a protean energy and an apparently insatiable appetite for work. If he received a critical drubbing he just shook the abuse from him like a shaggy dog, and moved on. He lived to direct and directed to live. I told him once that I wouldn't be directing anything new for nearly two years: 'I'd go mad', he said', but the combination of directing productions at the same time as being thoroughly on the case in every other department *is* a one-way ticket to the madhouse'.

Associate Director Michael Blakemore expressed concern (eventually in writing) about the lack of transparency over Hall's salary, still paid in full during his absences on outside work (unlike the Associate Directors); his royalties on transfers of National Theatre productions into the West End and on Broadway; his appointment of two assistants (who shared an agent with Peter Hall – Laurie Evans - and whose salaries were similarly not disclosed), and higher salaries for actors on Laurie Evans' books than for actors with other agents.

As Mr Blakemore indicated in his book *Stage Blood*: 'Peter was turning the organisation into a public-private partnership, where the government puts up the money and the unsupervised executives reward themselves with whatever sums they think fit'.

There was a messy dismissal/resignation (depending on whose memoirs you believe) and Michael departed - to enjoy on-going success with the RSC, and on Broadway. The National Theatre Board was forced to review the whole situation regarding agents, salaries, royalties, leave of absence for outside contracts &etc.

Richard Eyre's Diaries make more honest reading:
'If you run a theatre, there are only four decisions worth making: What play? Who will direct it? Who should be in it? Who should design it? Make that five decisions: Will anyone come to see it? To ignore that is to court disaster'. 'Creeping anxiety over next year's budget. I've learnt how difficult it is to control expenditure. It's partly the size of the auditoria, partly that if directors and designers see other successful productions with lavish sets they expect parity: it's the National Theatre, after all. I've got the very gravest fears about next year. I don't see where the successes will be. The biggest problem? Filling the Olivier'.

Klaus Völker's thoughts on post-war Germany's theatres:
'The brand new buildings are compromises between the artistic ambitions of the architects and the wishes of the municipal authorities. They induced the setting up of an enormous administrative machinery which has become a straightjacket for every kind of creative work in the theatre. Not one theatre building has been planned and built according to the ideas of the people who are working in it. Nearly 80% of the theatre's total budget is swallowed up by standing costs, so most of the monetary resources are used up before a single performance takes place. Each glass wall which has to be cleaned by window-cleaners makes inroads on the money which would otherwise go towards scenery and costumes'.

I remember the director of the (then) newly-opened Birmingham Repertory Theatre claiming that the annual window-cleaning bill for the new building was more than the combined rent and rates on the old theatre in Station Street. There are a great many 'windows' on the South Bank.

CHAPTER SEVENTEEN
HI-DIDDLE-DE, AN ACTOR'S LIFE FOR ME

A few items randomly gathered during research for this book:

Louise Brooks on Sarah Bernhardt:
Mr Pabst, my film director, had a photo of Sarah Bernhardt nude with a black-lace fan. In the twenties it was the custom for European actresses to send naked pictures of themselves to movie directors.

Moss Hart on Actors:
The general conception that all actors are born exhibitionists is far from the truth. They are quite the opposite. They are shy, frightened people hiding from themselves behind footlights, concealing their secret behind make-up and the characters they play. Their own self-rejection is what has made most of them actors. What better way to solve the problem than to be someone other than one's rejected self, and to be accepted and applauded for it every night? They have solved the problem – but not the torment. Which is what makes every opening night so painful an experience.

James Agate on Actors:
Greatness in acting requires a combination of things, not all of which are under the actor's control. Enough height, but not too much; beauty or, if not beauty, then the power to suggest it; brains and the ability to conceal them; physical health and the nervous system of an ox; indomitable spirit and natural grit; the flair for the right opportunity; luck or the knack of turning bad luck to account; a ruthless capacity to trample on all competing talents; *a complete lack of interest in the drama except in so far as it provides the actor with striking parts.* In addition to all this the great player, male or female, must possess that indefinable something which makes the ordinary man abase himself without knowing why.

James Agate on Paxinou:

Heard this story of the great Greek actress, Paxinou. On fire to play Mrs Alving she sent for the producer and made the proposal to him at the Savoy Hotel, coiled on a Louis Seize sofa *a la* Serpent-of-the-Nile and biting a flower *a la* Carmen, her arms cinct with diamond bracelets. Naturally he did not see her as Mrs Alving, and said so. 'Come to tea at my flat tomorrow' she commanded. Duly presenting himself, the flat door was opened by a dour, hard-faced creature with hair brushed back, totally lacking glamour. 'I want to see Madame Paxinou' said the producer, and received the reply 'I am Madame Paxinou - *as* Mrs Alving. *Now* do I play *Ghosts?*'

Ben Travers on Tom Walls:

Rehearsals of *A Cuckoo in the Nest* began five days after I had first met Tom Walls, and they gave me my first experience of some of his singular methods as actor-producer. For the first two of the three-week's rehearsal he sat and directed the rest of the company, including his understudy. At the beginning of the third week he resigned himself to participation in the acting. Of course he had been much too busy directing to study his own lines, and when the play started out on its one week probation at some provincial theatre his performance was liable to hiatus. This didn't embarrass him at all. He would cross to the prompt corner and rally the dithering stage manager with a rasping and resounding aside 'Come on, Bobbie, let's have it, can't you?' He had no shame or compunction about this.

He took a contemptuous view of audiences at the best of times, but it is only fair to say that on first nights in London he was not only word perfect but gave what was probably his best performance of the entire run. 'There's only one show that really matters' he used to say; a candid admission of his cynical outlook on the whole concern.

I wrote nine of the eleven farces produced at The Aldwych between 1925 and 1933. Tom Walls did not appear in the last two. If truth be told he did not appear at a good many performances of the others.

John Gielgud on Donald Wolfit:

I'd had enough of Hamlet by that time. I'd played a complete version, and a cut version and we'd moved to the West End, and I'd quarrelled with old Donald Wolfit who played the King and was very jealous and very stupid, and I didn't admire him at all although I thought he had great power. I didn't realise how much he resented me. I was of course rather conceited and vain and he probably had every right to resent me, but he did it rather unpleasantly, so he was rather a thorn in my flesh during the Hamlet times.

But he was very good as the King.

Peter Duguid (Corey) **on George Devine** (Darnforth):

I had never played with Devine before but found our first performance together (in *The Crucible*) the most exciting experience I've ever had as an actor. He was very generous to play with: absolute eye-to-eye tension. But after that one evening he never acted like that again.

There was only about 60% of him doing it. He'd come off talking about key lines, and make-up and somebody's wig-join. You could see that the cares of responsibility were with him even on stage.

Kenneth Tynan on Jerry Lewis:

At the Paris Olympia, Jerry Lewis opens to an audience including Aznavour, Bardot, etc. His finesse, his daintiness, his delicate mimetic skills are riveting. Cleverly adapting his act so that he avoids language (he speaks no French) he focusses on mime, song, gesture, dance, and miming to music, showing a command of vaudeville techniques such as I may never see again, and such as this audience has probably never seen before. Miming to a thirties big band record, he transforms its snarling riffs and growling trumpets into a bar-room brawl – *brilliant!*

Walter Winchell:

The American critic wrote 'In Hollywood they shoot too many pictures and not enough actors'.

After-Dinner Theatre:
There are, of course, many pleasant actors: you see their names on a cast list and know that you are going to have a happy week, or an enjoyable tour – but there are also several whom you would happily cross the road to avoid. During one of my Middle East residencies I flew over to Dubai to check out a Derek Nimmo touring production. As well as *All Gas and Gaiters* on TV and *Just a Minute* on radio Derek was also a very busy and very professional theatrical manager, sending out tours of top quality comedies on long tours through Australia, the Far East and the Middle East, performing as after-dinner theatre in the big hotel circuits. Dinner in the hotel ball-room, then the comedy on the ballroom platform or on a specially-erected stage.

His productions were always well presented, and very well cast: the one I was going to see was *Not Now Darling*, starring Leslie Phillips and David Jason. It took me a while to locate the company manager, and when I did eventually find him he was tearing his hair out. Apparently Leslie Phillips had a clause in his contract which said that his name should be above the title, and in larger letters than anyone else: the only other name on the publicity (below the title) being David Jason's. Mr Phillips had arrived in Dubai to discover that the hotel had printed all the posters and programmes with the two names side by side, above the title, in the same size lettering – and he hit the roof. 'No, that's not what we agreed. That's a clear breach of contract. I'm not doing the show: I'll go back to London if I have to, but I'm not doing the show'.

He sat in his hotel room, bags still packed, defiantly refusing to perform, while the poor company manager was desperately phoning Derek Nimmo; phoning Leslie Phillips' agent; negotiating with the hotel management in an attempt to find a solution. Meanwhile the ballroom was filling up with diners. Totally sold out: the audience didn't care a hoot about the size of the billing. I was among them, enjoying my meal: the only one in the packed dining room who knew that there might not be any *theatre* after the *dinner*.

With only a few minutes to spare the hotel manager agreed to reprint and redistribute all of the publicity the next morning, and Mr Phillips graciously agreed to perform. The exhausted Company Manager came and joined me at my table, staying just long-enough to start a round of applause on Leslie Phillips' first entrance (how he must have hated doing that) before disappearing – presumably to the bar.

I find all that absolutely unforgivable: whatever the legalities of the occasion (and they could be sorted out later, in London, by lawyers) you don't put your colleagues out of work on a whim; you don't deny a performance to a Full House, already in their seats.

From the memoirs of the two actors involved:

David Jason in 'My Life'.
'I have done three tours for Derek Nimmo: two were pretty much unalloyed joy from start to finish: the third starred Leslie Phillips.
The tour was already under way when I was flown out to replace Andrew Sachs who was about to start work on *Fawlty Towers*. It was planned that I'd rehearse during the last fortnight in Australia, and take over the part in Singapore. Most of the first week I rehearsed with the stage manager. At last, Friday afternoon, Leslie finally appears.
'I'm going to be whispering' he whispers.
'Sorry?' I say.
'I'm going to be whispering' Leslie whispers.
'I'm sorry, I can't hear you. You're whispering'.
'I have to save my voice for the play'.
'OK'.
Although, inside, I'm thinking 'This is not great'.
Off we go, me talking, Leslie whispering. We reach a point in the play where I'm standing centre stage with Leslie and he turns his back to me and addresses one of the other characters. It all goes rather quiet for me at this point, now that I can't see his whispering lips; I miss my cue and have no idea what's going on.

The show opens in Singapore with me feeling frighteningly unrehearsed. Leslie has everybody going at breakneck speed: everything is flying at me so quickly I don't know whether it's Tuesday or a lemon. Come the fourth night I've started to settle in a bit, getting laughs where there hadn't been laughs before – much to Leslie's confusion. From Jakarta on, there's a bit of a thaw in relations, and our relationship becomes workable. I'm glad I stuck at it: the audiences were wonderful'.

and Leslie Phillips in 'Hello'.
'I ran into David Jason at Ronnie and Joy Barker's annual party. Twenty years earlier David and I had toured all over the world with *Not Now Darling*: nothing bonds actors like a foreign tour'.

In that same chapter, whilst on tour in Australia Mr Phillips is told of the death of his first wife Penny in a fire. 'Obviously there was no way I could leave the production to attend the funeral – I *was* the show. If I went, they would have to close the production, an awful lot of people would be badly let down, and I would be sued'.

Final thoughts:

Alan Bennett on Christopher Plummer:
He's his own worst enemy – but only just.

Bernard Shaw on Actors:
Discussing a play with an actor is a rash experiment, not to be lightly attempted.

CHAPTER EIGHTEEN
THE POSTMAN COMETH

When Eugene O'Neill's play *The Iceman Cometh* was running in the West End I heard Edith Evans giving a poetry recital on the radio. She included this:
Whether the Iceman cometh or not,
bothers me not one jot.
But what does bother me a lot,
is that the Postman cometh not.

In 1963, when I was touring India with the Bristol Old Vic Company - as their technician, not as an actor - the director, Denis Carey, realised he was short of understudies and threw me a script. 'Read that' he said, so I did. He listened for a couple of minutes then said 'You can't act'. It didn't worry me: I had no ambitions to be an actor. Ambitions, yes. To be an actor, absolutely not.

So often in my life I've been reminded that I'm not much good at anything. One afternoon during summer term at my Grammar School the Religious Education master threw me a cricket ball and watched my first-ever attempt to bowl it at the far stumps. The first attempt was also my last. I didn't actually think it was all that wide: he thought it was, and dispatched me to the athletics track. My first mile took over ten minutes, and I was then transferred from the track to the field – and handed a javelin. An odd piece of equipment, I thought, for a boy who couldn't aim a cricket ball.

I had to leave the Grammar School at age fifteen when my father contracted tuberculosis, so I was spared the inevitable embarrassments of University. I might, perhaps, have avoided the games field, but my admitted lack of communication skills would have made university life pretty miserable. I had good parents: somehow we five children (of whom I was the eldest) were always fed and clothed and educated even during the war years, but there was no culture, little conversation and no consultation.

Dad was already in the hospital before we were told what was wrong with him: any family problems were discussed after we had gone to bed. As an example, my dog disappeared a few days before we moved house; I still don't know whether he was put down or taken to a dog's home.

The result was that I became a bit of a loner, and got used to working out my own personal solutions to any problems rather than talking them through with a better-informed adult – or even a fellow scholar. I never had any problems with figures, with mathematics - a logical science suited to loners who had to think things out for themselves – but the art of 'debating' was alien to me. Arguing for the sake of it, adopting an attitude (especially one in opposition to your real beliefs) seemed pointless. I did the debating in my own head; sorted out the logical solution, and acted on it. All of which made me a rotten companion: I had very little to say, and what I did say always sounded opinionated.

I would have been side-lined at University although it is just possible, I suppose, that I might have got involved with drama sooner than I did, and that the processes of design and rehearsal would have forced me to be more expansive; to explain to others the reasoning behind my *logical production decisions*. Much more likely (and reasonable?) might have been 'you did Physics, Maths and Applied Maths; what do you know about theatre?

My early years in show business were mostly spent learning the technical side of theatrical production, and then being told 'you can't do that' when I wanted to move into management. 'What do you know about theatre management; you're a technician'. I took some time out to do an Arts Admin. degree course at Central London Polytechnic which helped for a while but the next time I tried to move on it was 'what do you know about directing; you're a theatre manager'. And then 'what do you know about script-writing, you're a director'.

The playwright John Whiting had similar problems when his first play *Saint's Day* was greeted by a howl of derision. His reaction was 'I suppose there have been people who have actually given up the theatre and not written any more plays because the critics said they couldn't do it. People have always said that I can't do it. Perhaps I can't. But I do. It's a compulsive thing'. He went on *to find his tambourine,* and to write *The Devils.*

Was I lonely? Possibly. But not too unhappy with the situation, perhaps for a reason which I did not appreciate early on and which was only diagnosed during National Service when it became clear that I couldn't read radio signals whenever there was background static on the line. To this day I cannot make out what radio announcers are saying if there is background music playing. Crowds make me deaf: I can be in a busy restaurant and not pick out a single word of what the person next to me is saying because of the background noise. Discos and pop concerts were a nightmare: I could hear the percussion only too well, but couldn't make out one word of the lyrics. And I couldn't chat up whoever I had gone with. Or anyone I wanted to leave with. Which brings us to the one subject carefully avoided in my memoir, *Meanderings: A River and a Life.* Sex. Avoided largely because there wasn't much of it anyway, and because what little there was would not have made very interesting reading. To be honest, sex was just another of those things which I wasn't very good at. It started late and, for better or worse, finished early.

Why? I'm not sure. An outsider who understood himself but didn't *like* himself, perhaps? Not strong on personal relationships, for a variety of reasons of which sex was only one. I was certainly confused by the subject: we had no sex education, at home or school or church. No internet, no porn channels - just well-worn copies of Hank Jansen paperbacks bringing us to the brink without going into sufficient detail. The Grammar School was all-boys, which added to the confusion.

I remember strolling round the playing field during breaks with a slim, sandy-haired fourth-year named Fletcher. I don't remember what we talked about. In my innocence I wasn't even aware that we might have had things to talk about. If Fletcher was aware, then he never mentioned it. If we had, who knows? Maybe my life might have taken a different direction. Then again, maybe not. When I did eventually discover what we might have talked about I also discovered that it was illegal; that it could lead to imprisonment and to extremely public vilification, muddying the deepening sexual waters even further. A 'loner' doesn't need all these complications.

Meanwhile, life was changing all around me: we had Rock'n'Roll, coffee bars and the swinging sixties. National Service and, later, three summers at Butlin's brought me an increased awareness of loosening sexual morals, but also an increasing realisation that I still had a great deal to learn. Not having a settled home base was always a major drawback: you can't settle down with anyone unless you have somewhere to settle. Much of my career was spent on tour, both within Britain and abroad. I never had a 'home' of my own until I swapped touring for an enjoyable eight-year Scottish residency managing theatres in Stirling and Kirkcaldy. Until then relationships were mostly short-term, often within the touring theatre company, and usually finishing with the end of the tour.

We are, I think, still on the subject of sex. Love was a strange concept for a loner: the idea of combining a travelling life (and no home base) with a committed relationship 'till death us do part' was never a realistic possibility. Not even a desirable possibility: as the eldest of five children I had already had my fill of puking infants, and nappy-changing, and baby-sitting. I certainly had no intention of going through all that again, a decision made easier by my long-held conviction that over-population will, either directly or indirectly, eventually end life as we know it on this planet.

Watching my parents struggle to hold the home together
(particularly during dad's illness and convalescence)
convinced this logical loner that family life wasn't for me. I
wouldn't have coped well with the responsibilities of a long-
term relationship, and what my dad called *a proper job*. When
Olivier offered me the post at the National dad's response was
'Isn't it time you gave all this up and got a proper job?' By
which he meant bank clerk, or an accountant of some kind.
For me, signing up to a mortgage and a lifetime of 'decorating
and gardening' was never an option.

Once you discount procreation and romance, sex becomes a
lesser driving force: more *lust* than *love*; the child at the
sweetie counter screaming 'I want'. An occasional cure for
loneliness, perhaps, but for the most part, it was 'end of tour:
end of affair'. No tears, no great sense of loss or
disappointment. With just one exception: Khalid. At first
meeting, a slim, attractive 21-year-old Indian living in New
Delhi. A talented young actor, he had been engaged by the
British Council to liaise with our touring company during our
1978 stay in his city. Sunday lunchtime he turned up at our
hotel with two tickets for a Gallery Preview, and invited me
to join him. Throughout the afternoon we talked non-stop
about almost everything but pictures: an unusual experience
for a loner. Since then we have met only five times but
continue to correspond. The correspondence halted during his
first marriage, to a Polish actress, but picked up again
following her sad death from cancer after we discovered that
we had each been checking out the other's website.

For me, Khalid is a little like a child's 'imaginary friend';
always 'there' despite not being 'here'. Real, in a way that the
imaginary friend never could be, and we had the postman to
keep us in touch. Our friendship was reminiscent of Bernard
Shaw's 'courtship by correspondence' with the actress Ellen
Terry. Shaw said that he fell madly in love with her when he
saw her on stage, but was fearful of materialising their
friendship with an actual meeting. 'The perfect love affair is
one which is conducted by post' wrote Shaw.

Bernard Shaw celebrated his 29th birthday with a *new experience*. Mrs Jenny Paterson, a widow and a singing pupil of his mother, invited him to supper. 'I was no sooner inside her door than she put her arms around me and said she adored me. Being intensely curious on the subject, I let her get on with it'. He admitted to later affairs with actresses and with unattached female members of the Fabian Society; although his marriage to Charlotte (née Payne-Townsend) apparently *owed nothing at all to sexual passion*. Late in life, however, he suggested that despite all these *affairs* he had only actually *been in love* twice: once in his youth, and once in his middle age. He mentioned no names but, since he also differentiates between *lust* and *love* I suggest possibly Matthew Edward McNulty, a schoolboy friend with whom he wrote, and played piano duets, and continued a correspondence for over 70 years, and Harley Granville-Barker whose second wife hated Shaw and insisted on their exodus to France, and who also carried on a lifetime of correspondence published as the *Shaw-Barker Letters*.

My last actual meeting with Khalid was in 1991 during what I guessed would be my final tour of the sub-continent when, at his late father's invitation, I stayed briefly at their lovely family home in Delhi. A home designed for 'settling-down' and Khalid has recently done that again with Kasia, another Polish lady - this time a film director – after a longish engagement. Their wedding photos arrived by email: our friendship has survived through into the digital age. Such a warm, close and continuing friendship, even without 'materialisation', has proved a great boost to self-confidence.

Another great boost has been provided by Professor John Pick's *coffee morning tutorials*. John attended one of my Talks (to a local branch of the WI) and said 'you *can* do that': he read some of my magazine articles and scripts and said 'you *can* do that'. After years of supposed inadequacy, these various encouragements have helped this *loner* to become more confident, more out-going, having at last discovered things he can do – and apparently do quite well.

The ill-educated non-communicator has *found his tambourine*, started to *like* himself, and is enjoying his 'third age' – but that's for a later chapter. Meanwhile, the erudite 21-year-old graduate Khalid is now a 62-year-old visiting professor, a drama teacher, an occasional film actor and solo stage performer. I enjoyed one of his shows, *Foolsong*, when he visited London many years ago, and I have seen a video of a recent Polish television film (directed by his wife) showing his detailed preparations for *Cut Flowers*, his third such solo presentation. A true craftsman (he also designs and makes furniture) and *preparation* involves the design and manufacture of all his own props and costumes.

He was staggered to hear that one of my recent tours had thirteen performances in nine days, and involved four different scripts. 'You're a performing maniac' he wrote. 'I couldn't cope with that kind of schedule'. Unless his work brings him to London it is unlikely that we shall meet again: our friendship, however, remains the most important relationship of my life and I trust and hope that he will find time between rehearsals and teaching and writing and performing to click SEND occasionally.

In his maturity, the Australian author Patrick White wrote 'you reach a point where you have had everything, and everything amounts to nothing. Only love redeems. The love shared with an individual - not necessarily sexual, seductive though sexuality may be. Or is this a straw grabbed at by an ageing man as passion flows out of reach? If it is *making do* then let us make do, whatever our age, in a world falling apart'.

Should Khalid ever make it to England I'll insist on him meeting Mary G Evans (I've never asked her what the G stands for). I first met Mary in 1966: she was on the stage management team of Scottish Opera when I joined them as touring electrician with responsibility for reproducing Charles Bristow's atmospheric lighting in the various touring venues.

Scottish Opera, a touring company, was in its fifth season when I joined them: the driving force of the entire operation being maestro Alexander Gibson (*below*). His companions in the pit were the formidable Scottish National Orchestra. Our 1966 tour visited Glasgow, Edinburgh and Aberdeen with a revival of *Faust* alongside new productions of *Falstaff, Die Walküre* (the first part of Artistic Director Peter Ebert's eventual full Ring Cycle) and Britten's *Albert Herring*.

Albert Herring had a near-perfect cast, most of them with experience of Britten's operas in London and Aldeburgh. Gregory Dempsey in the title role may have been under his mother's thumb but was certainly not a *mother's boy*, and clearly ready to break loose at the first opportunity.

With superb atmospheric sets by Adam Pollock, and impeccable direction by Anthony Besch, *Albert Herring* represented Britain (and Britten) at dozens of foreign music festivals (usually with the same cast) and remained in the repertoire almost as long as their wonderful *Tosca*.

I returned to Scottish Opera in 1967 when the tour started with their first visit to Perth for two nights of *Albert Herring*, and the premiere performances of *Cosi fan Tutte* in a translation by Ruth and Thomas Brown, the best version I have seen. John Stoddart's brilliantly-original setting for Act One was the  Turkish Baths, with the three male principals all in towels or dressing gowns. What better setting for a group of men to discuss the vagaries of women?

The production toured to Glasgow, Aberdeen and Edinburgh with new productions of *La Bohème* (in those ingenious sets by Peter Rice), *Das Rheingold*, and a revival of *Otello*. The day before the dress rehearsal of *Otello* the lighting designer, Charles Bristow, asked me to meet him at lunchtime in the 'office' (the pub next door) where he explained that he had been unexpectedly summoned back to Sadlers Wells. Would I do the lighting for *Otello?*

'I've cleared it with the management, if you're agreeable'.

'When are you off?'

'Two o'clock train. Here are the plans'.

It had been a while since I had designed lighting for anything, and I had never lit an opera. Suddenly I was landed with an opera I didn't know, in sets I had never seen, with the dress rehearsal the following evening. Basically the setting was open stage, just one huge (Ralph Koltai) ramp. It's always easier to light shows if there's no scenery getting in the way, and I was reasonably satisfied with the end result. Stage management advised on the reasons for, and the timings of, the various lighting changes. We got by, but it was a relief to have Charles back in time for the Wagner. An odd experience, but it means that I can now claim to have done the lighting for both Sir Laurence Olivier's *Othello* and Sir Charles Craig's *Otello*.

Now, how did we get onto opera? Oh yes, Mary G Evans. She'd been deputy stage manager on the first of those tours and impressed everyone with her efficiency, and an ability to see the funny side of most situations. GSOH in the days before GSOH was common parlance. The singer Phyllis Curtin was in the company, and I heard Mary on the tannoy 'Miss Curtin, your call, please'. She then turned to me and said 'I suppose you could say that was a *curtin call*'. We've been friends ever since.

We both returned to London at the end of our contracts. I had been invited by Anthony Besch (impressed with my efforts on *Otello?*) to stage manage and light an opera double bill at the Camden Festival (with Roger Norrington as MD).

Mary joined Peter Brook as his personal assistant - it runs in the family: her mother was, for a while, PA to Mrs Patrick Campbell. I enjoyed my occasional visits to her parent's Bedfordshire home: sadly my last such visit was for her father's funeral. Mary and I have kept in touch over the years –although not without the occasional misunderstanding; her handwriting was (still is) pretty to look at but difficult to read: I remember one letter telling me that she was looking after Peter Brook's horse while he was away, and I wondered where one stabled a horse in London. Turned out she was looking after his house. Emails have removed some – but not all – of the guesswork.

She went off to Paris with Peter Brook when he set up his International Centre of Theatre Research at the Bouffes du Nord, and travelled with them on their tours through Persia, in the Sahara, and to Brooklyn. Back in Britain she settled in Exeter as PA to the Artistic Director at the Northcott Theatre and later, with Monica Shallis (a talented voice, drama and music teacher), they set up the Cygnet Training Theatre – eventually in their own custom-built venue. Cygnet is still flourishing, despite Monica's sad demise a few years back.

My post-tambourine career takes me down to Devon several times a year, offering opportunities for fun meals with the still-smiling Mary. Khalid's photo also shows still-smiling eyes. I suspect that they might get on well together.

CHAPTER NINETEEN
AROUND THE WORLD IN EIGHTY PLAYS

My theatre work has taken me to forty-three different countries, including eight tours of the Indian sub-continent, three residencies in the Middle East, and two trips right around the world, as well as periods working with some of Britain's leading theatre companies. However, my first foreign trip wasn't theatrical but military: my second year of National Service was spent in Hong Kong.

At the end of a year-long Mandarin Chinese course, we flew out to Hong Kong on a BOAC Argonaut with stops in Rome, Basrah, Patna, and Singapore. In Basrah we stayed overnight at the Shat-al-Arab Hotel: even at that time relations with the Iraqis were a little tense so we had been told to travel in civilian clothes in the hope that no-one would guess that we thirty young men with short-back-and-sides haircuts were servicemen – but we may have given the game away when we checked into the hotel wearing our civvies, but carrying all our gear in grey RAF kitbags with our names and numbers stencilled down the side.

The first foreign adventure under 'my own management' was to Germany: you'll remember that I had moved to the Aldwych Theatre to work with the Royal Shakespeare Company. Colleagues there told me about the impressive new post-war German theatres with their superb modern technical equipment, so I used my first paid holiday to hitch-hike around Germany checking out these amazing buildings. I had heard that some of the stages were so big you had to drive from one side to the other – and almost believed it when I saw a mini drive out through the scene dock doors as I arrived at the Cologne Opera House. I was made welcome everywhere; sometimes even offered accommodation by the theatre staff. The buildings themselves were spectacular, and the equipment way in advance of ours with rolling stages and huge lighting desks.

I was able to see performances at almost every venue, with some spectacular – and highly-technical – stage settings and scene changes, but suspected (no more than a gut feeling really - remember, I was still quite new to the business) that we probably used our older British equipment to slightly better *artistic* effect. I experienced the long coach ride across (then-still-closed) Eastern Germany to West Berlin with its incredible new Opera House – and then through the Wall, only to be turned away from the East Berlin Opera House: 'closed: come back in the autumn'.

A wasted trip? Not at all – I had a much more important appointment in East Berlin. A visit to Bertolt Brecht's theatre on the Kurfurstendamm where Helene Weigel welcomed me, and took me through to watch a rehearsal of *The Good Women of Setzuan*. Four years in the repertoire and still rehearsing! In the foyer they had a case-full of books about Brecht from all over the world, and I was happy to donate Eric Bentley's biography of Brecht which had been part of my reading on the trip. I had to get back through the Wall, so sadly couldn't see a performance, but an unforgettable experience.

(Helene Weigel as Mother Courage)

One of the founder members of both the RSC and the National Theatre was an eccentric Irish-born actor and former revue artist Max Adrian, with whom I had worked in both

organisations. Max was responsible for my first round-the-world tour, as stage manager for his one-man-show *An Evening with George Bernard Shaw*, put together from a selection of Shaw's letters and newspaper reviews. We opened with a couple of performances in Auckland, and then headed for Australia.

We were met at Sydney airport by an Australian Arts Council official who pointed out the main attractions as we drove into the city. 'That's the Quantas Hotel' he said, unfortunately adding 'where the big stars stay when they're in Sydney'. The car didn't stop, and I felt the temperature cooling rapidly as we drove on, over the famous bridge and on up into North Sydney, stopping at a Motel just round the corner from the theatre where we would be performing. A Motel chosen for our convenience – but not suitable for an actor who had been a founder member of both the National Theatre and the Royal Shakespeare Company, with his name in lights on Broadway for playing Pangloss in the original production of Leonard Bernstein's *Candide*. At 7.30 the next morning Max was sitting in the Motel foyer, bags packed, waiting for a taxi to take him to the Quantas Hotel 'where the big stars stay when they are in Sydney'.

These attempts to cope with the vagaries of (usually) older, experienced 'stars', remind me of Ronald Harwood's play (and film) *The Dresser*. Nothing on that scale with Max, fortunately, but sometimes little things lead to frustration. For instance, Max was consistently early for every engagement: I would get the theatre all set up, then dash back to the hotel allowing half-an-hour for a shower and a cup of tea before the agreed time to drive him to the theatre, only to find him already waiting in the lobby. His show had GBS at three different ages involving three sets of wigs, beards, eye-brows and moustaches: he developed a skin rash which he blamed on the Australian spirit gum. I had some British spirit gum flown out by the British Council, but the rash had cleared up before it arrived. So I wasn't convinced by the ending of *The Dresser* when 'Sir' dies quietly at the end of his performance and his wife and dresser have a quiet sympathetic drink together before the curtain falls. A cop-out, I'm afraid: in reality, there's no death: they would both go off to their separate beds in the certain knowledge that tomorrow they would be going through exactly the same routine all over again – and tomorrow – and tomorrow. *That* is show business.

 We had afternoon tea in the waterside home of another big star, Googie Withers, probably now best-remembered for the TV series *Within These Walls*. Her husband John McCallum had been Joint Managing Director of J C Williamson Theatres, but at the time of our visit was producing the second *Skippy* series for Australian TV. They still did theatre work, in Australia and Britain, and were currently appearing together in the first Australian production of an Alan Ayckbourn play, *Relatively Speaking*. Our performance times clashed, so we couldn't see each other's shows, and afternoon tea was the only chance for the 'old-timers' to meet and catch up. Googie told us about their preview night with *Relatively Speaking* when the curtains got caught on the footlights. Half went up while, 'with a terrible tearing noise' the other half fell down. 'A ripping good night' reported the local paper.

That tour took us to Australia's oldest working theatre, the 1836 Theatre Royal in Hobart, Tasmania, built partly with convict labour. Noel Coward appeared there, and called it 'a dream of a theatre' but by the 1940s it was in a poor state. Demolition seemed likely until the recently-knighted Sir Laurence Olivier, on tour with an Old Vic Company, made an impassioned speech from the stage which encouraged the State Government to buy and renovate the building.

I think it's fair to say that Australia is not the most cultured of countries: we did the show in an Arts Centre in Mildura, in South Australia: set in a park in a bend of the river with vineyards stretching into the distance. I said to someone in the town the next morning 'I think you've got the nicest little theatre we've seen anywhere in Australia'. 'Have we got a theatre?' he said. 'I didn't know we had a theatre: we've got the longest bar in the world. It's in the Guinness Book of Records' and he took me to see it. A long saloon with a bar counter that started at one end, ran almost the complete length of the room before horse-shoeing round and heading back to the starting wall. The longest bar counter in the world.

We certainly had a great time out there, and met some wonderful people, but I do sometimes find myself remembering Australia as the longest bar in the world.

Next stop, Singapore: I had been there only once before, on my way home from National Service in Hong Kong. The Mandarin Chinese learnt during my first year of National Service

has twice proved advantageous during my theatre career: I toured Britain as manager with a Peking Opera Company from Shanghai playing several dates on tour and a week at the London Coliseum, but my biggest thrill was actually to go into China, as a stage manager with London Festival Ballet, running the prompt corner in Mandarin and giving cues to the local technicians. A week in Beijing and a week in Shanghai. London Festival Ballet was only the second foreign company to be allowed in after Mao's cultural revolution so this was a long time ago, before the country had opened up to tourists and foreign capital. Everyone, men and women, still wore those loose blue boiler suits, and there was hardly a car to be seen on the roads, just bicycles ten deep and ten abreast at every junction.

We were followed everywhere by crowds who had not seen foreigners, or spoken English, for twenty years. One elderly man was too nervous to be seen talking to me face to face, and we conversed over our shoulders: his English was rusty, but fluent. My most vivid memory is of a little girl, four or five years old, suddenly looking up and seeing a group of us, dancers and technicians, and running screaming to her father, absolutely petrified; hugging his legs, and occasionally risking a look to check that the foreign devils weren't coming to get her. Her first-ever sight of a non-Oriental face.

On a later Far East tour with the London Shakespeare Group we took a production of *Romeo & Juliet* to Japan. Trying to squeeze in as much Japanese theatre as possible during our nine days in Tokyo I went to matinees, late night shows and two shows on the Sunday (our free day), fitting in eight productions around our own evening performances. Some were traditional; Kabuki and puppets: one was bizarre – a huge, Palladium-style song-and-dance spectacular but with an all-female cast, half of them in 'drag'. Slick, professional and totally sold out. The show which made the greatest impression on me, however, was a contemporary production in a packed, sweltering basement theatre on the theme of the manipulation of talent by Svengali-like directors and managers. I confess that I didn't pick up all of the references, but Monroe, Garland and Nijinsky were certainly in there. Wonderful imagery from both performers and designers.

During my spell of management at the Adam Smith Theatre in Kirkcaldy we hosted a charming and talented Japanese children's theatre company, *Himawari*. I had seen them in Edinburgh in 1986, and immediately made it clear to Visiting Arts that we wanted them should they be touring again in Britain. They used no make-up or props, no sound tapes, no musical instruments and only a few spoken words (in both English and Japanese) and they performed three Grimm's Tales using just simple costumes and tremendous imagination as they became horses, bears, princes, furniture – and even a lake-full of swans. They returned in 1989; we were on their itinerary, and they were a delight. In a rare burst of generosity the Council gave them a Civic Reception, and a tour of the Council Chamber.

Three of my most exciting evenings in the theatre were the amazing Yukio Ninagawa shows brought to Edinburgh for the Festivals: *Macbeth* (1985) at the Lyceum; *Medea* – out-doors in the Adam Courtyard of the University (1986), and a gigantic *Tempest* (1988) overflowing from Edinburgh's largest stage, at the Playhouse: in my front row seat my knees were underneath their forestage and I had an uncluttered view as Ariel flew from tree to tree, and arriving boats disgorged their passengers.

The next leg of Max's GBS tour took us to India, one of my eight tours of that sub-continent. The first had been in 1963 with a Bristol Old Vic company directed by Denis Carey. We took three plays, Shakespeare's *Hamlet*, Robert Bolt's *A Man for All Seasons*, and Shaw's first comedy *Arms and the Man* to East and West Pakistan, India and Ceylon as they were then known. We left London Airport on Boxing Day 1962 only hours before blizzards closed down not just Heathrow but most of Britain. Nowadays these touring companies stay in the best hotels, travel in air-conditioned jet planes and perform in modern, well-equipped theatres. For that 1963 tour, however, performances were often in school halls or railway institutes, and internal flights were in the old Dakota DC3s left over from the war, the mainstay of Indian Airlines at that time. Conditions did improve slowly over those eight tours. It wasn't all work: we did some touristy things: we saw the Taj Mahal, for instance – which really is as stunning as everyone says, and theatrical in a way since you don't enter directly into those incredible gardens, but through a dark narrow corridor suddenly emerging into the glare, rather like the curtain going up in a darkened theatre to reveal the dazzlingly-lit setting beyond. Unforgettable.

In Bombay (now Mumbai) we took the boat across to Elephanta Island, and climbed the thousand steps to the impressive temple with the giant phallic statues. We experienced thrilling train rides climbing from Bombay up to Poona, and from Colombo up to Kandy, with the track hugging the edges of the mountains: thick jungle rising to one side: a 500 foot drop on the other.

Strangely though, it's the silly little things that stick in the memory – the rudimentary Dacca hotel where, if you needed hot water for a shave or a bath, you called down from the balcony, and bearers would heat up buckets on an open fire in the courtyard below.
The monkey in the Madras Music Academy which sat in the roof girders high above the stage piddling down on the scenery and actors below. *Romeo and Juliet*: that's quite a long piddle.
An after-show reception in Delhi when the Deputy High Commissioner's wife served us sausage and mash and baked beans which she had ordered especially from London because, as she said, 'I thought you might be getting a bit bored with chicken curry and rice'.

A bigger memory: flying in a tiny Fokker Friendship plane up the valleys towards Katmandu in Nepal. The Fokker Friendships had the wings on top so you had incredibly clear views through all of the windows of the mountains rising on each side, bright green from the steeply-terraced paddy fields. Then, as the plane rounded the final peak, through all of the starboard windows you had the unmistakable sight of Mount Everest in the distance.

These tours were arranged by the British Council, an organisation responsible for the promotion abroad of British Culture and the English language: largely funded by the Foreign Office despite (in theory) operating independently of Embassies or High Commissions. The British Council staff were mainly professionals; teachers, agriculturists, scientists rather than Foreign Office recruits.

The greatest character I ever met, anywhere, was David Horsburgh, who worked for the British Council in Madras. David had been a professor of English in Mysore before joining the Council, and he had a passion for education. Not the 'lines of desks in front of a teacher' type of education, but a school to which pupils went because they  wanted to, and not because they 'jolly-well-had-to'. A school with no rules, no failures, no punishments.

In 1972 he told his wife Doreen that they were going to open their own little school. 'Yes, dear', she said. Up in the jungle, at Neel Bagh. 'Yes, dear'. David had found *his tambourine*: he built the schoolroom himself, an Indian-style hut with floors made of polished, beaten cow dung. They started with just two students; village boys. More village children soon enrolled, boys and girls, aged from five to fifteen. No exams, no classes, no grades. There was a timetable, but with the whole school working together on the same subject, albeit at different levels and speeds.

'Like a family or village', said David, 'with the younger ones absorbing the knowledge and experience of the older students'. That timetable included the village language Telegu; the state language Kannada; the national language Hindi – and English. Their knowledge of English was sufficiently fluent to permit full productions of Shakespeare plays. When I visited the school on what I suspected would be my final tour of India, there were some thirteen-year-olds taking part in their seventh such Shakespeare production. Other subjects included Maths, Science, Environmental Studies, Arts and Crafts, Philosophy and Music. David financed all this by writing books for Oxford University Press. He died in 1984 and I was privileged to attend a memorial service in London: a full house for a very special man. If there is a heaven, David will certainly be there.

Without doubt, the highest point of my Indian experiences was an unexpected meeting at Bombay's open-air swimming pool with Geoffrey Kendal and Laura Liddell. You may remember them as the stars of the Merchant-Ivory film *Shakespeare-Wallah*, although nowadays they are probably better-remembered as the parents of that lovely actress Felicity Kendal. According to Felicity, in their early twenties her parents were very much in love with their work and with each other: a lifelong partnership that was indestructible.

Like William Poel, Geoffrey's productions cut down on scenery and relied largely on the spoken word. I was then doing for just three months at a time, what the Kendals had done for twenty years or more: touring scaled-down productions of classical British drama to the schools, colleges, towns and cities of the Indian sub-continent, but with the enormous difference that they did it all on their own initiative and at their own expense, whereas we were getting salaries, hotel accommodation, transport and administration all provided by the British Council.

They had worked in Repertory theatres in Britain before forming their own touring company. Geoffrey served in the Merchant Navy at the start of the war but was transferred to ENSA, and it was an ENSA tour of the thriller *Gaslight* which first took them to India. The Bombay army officer in charge of the tour was the actor Jack Hawkins. ENSA had provided costumes without linings, believing that they would be cooler in the hot climate. In fact, without linings, the costumes got saturated with perspiration, getting blacker and blacker as the evenings wore on. Despite their many problems, including bouts of fever, they did 86 shows on that first tour and never missed a performance.

One of their colleagues, Peter Meriton, suggested that they might return to India after the war with a small company similar to the ENSA troupe playing scenes from Shakespeare in colleges and schools, and in December 1946 they did exactly that, travelling out first class on P&O liner Strathmore for £70 a head. The 'heads' by then included daughter Jennifer, a thirteen-year-old actress, and the new-born baby Felicity. Their tours would take them all over the sub-continent.

Their most disastrous experience was on the way back from performances in Manipur when one of their land rovers was swept away while attempting to cross a swollen river late at night. The driver, who couldn't swim, was washed downstream but fortunately managed to catch hold of the branches of a submerged tree, and was rescued. The next morning a British Army crane hauled the sunken land rover out of the river, but everything in it had been spirited away during the night, including clothes, money, travellers' cheques and account books. They were forced to remain in that area performing *Arms and the Man* on tea estates and in Planters Clubs until they had replenished their finances.

On my own Indian tours we performed in many of their old venues: the London Shakespeare Group, like the Kendals before us, performed in the tiny Gaiety Theatre up in the hills in the summer capital of Simla. The last Viceroy of India, Earl Mountbatten saw amateur performances of Gilbert & Sullivan at the Gaiety, but it had 'gorn down' a bit since his time: we actually had to sweep the theatre *and the seats* before we dared open the doors to the audience. The beautiful

 little auditorium has happily since been restored to its former Imperial splendour.

The Kendal's elder daughter Jennifer married a young Indian member of their touring company, Shashi Kapoor, who later became a huge Bollywood star. The couple settled in Juhu, north of Bombay, raised three children, and built their own theatre – the Prithvi Theatre named after Shashi's famous actor-father. On one of my later tours, with *Kemp's Jig*, a one-man show starring Chris Harris as Will Kemp, he performed at the Prithvi Theatre and another of the Kendal's venues, the Dehra Dun School north of Delhi. So many shared memories: for instance we had all worked in Pune (then known as Poona): for our performances there with *Dear Liar* we stayed at the Pune Club, and dined in its wonderful restaurant – the tall bearers splendid in turbans, red sashes over their starched white uniforms: every table laid with starched white linen and cut-glass crystal - and only four of us dining. For their performances in Pune the Kendals had engaged a hotel dhobi to iron their *Othello* costumes. He took great care - rather too much care, said Laura - and at the half-hour call he was being hurried along by anxious half-naked actors who sorted the remaining costumes in the order of their various appearances, but he was still ironing well into the first act. Geoffrey, as Othello, was in full flow in the first jealousy scene, when the dhobi suddenly appeared on stage, his bundled-up iron on his head, and shook hands with Othello saying 'All done now, sahib, I am thanking you' – before departing.

Jennifer's younger sister Felicity was cast in a leading role alongside her parents in the 1963 film *Shakespeare-Wallah* the start of a successful career on both stage and television.

We have never worked together (yet), but Felicity kindly checked the Indian chapters in my memoir *Meanderings: A River and a Life,* for which I remain most grateful.

The Indians know, and love, Shakespeare: their education syllabus, even after Independence, was still based on the 'Singapore Papers, the Commonwealth version of the Cambridge 'O' and 'A' levels, and their English set texts always included Shakespeare. Many new rulers of former colonial countries avoided official Embassy or High Commission functions although they were more relaxed about attending cultural events. Pandit Nehru had enjoyed several of the Kendals' shows at the Gaiety Theatre in Simla and, on our 1963 Bristol Old Vic tour, that same Pandit Nehru, by then Prime Minister, was the guest of the British Council at the opening night of *Hamlet* in New Delhi.

We have similarly welcomed Mrs Ghandi in India, Mrs Banderanaika in Sri Lanka, the President of China and the Crown Prince of Nepal, but my outstanding memory is of the Emir of Kano, in Northern Nigeria. He came to the show, turned up unexpectedly at the British Council reception afterwards and he then invited us all to his Palace for an *official audience* the following morning. The *Palace* was

basically a single-storey building with battlements, but the interior was fantastic. The throne room had a huge ornate throne at one end and a long row of chairs down each side, where we sat waiting. He made an entrance that Dame Edna Everage would have envied, wearing his full Emiri court dress, all gold cloth, including a sash, a huge turban and those shoes with the curled-up toes which I'd only seen before in productions of Aladdin. We sat in official audience for about twenty minutes, asking about his state, his country, and his role in it, and then he said 'Wait while I get out of these things, and we'll go and have a drink'.

A Moslem Emir, remember, but he did enjoy a gin-and-tonic.

At the end of one Indian tour I had permission to stay on for a few days and I flew up to Kabul in Afghanistan for a brief holiday, returning on one of those ramshackle buses crammed inside and on top with boxes and trunks, bedding rolls and chickens, travelling all the way down through the Khyber Pass and back to Peshawar. On the way, the bus stopped at the famous market at Landi Kotal where, among the usual spread-blankets with their vegetables, fabrics and spices you could buy any kind of hard drug, and every imaginable kind of weapon from a tank to a Kalashnikov, together with the ammunition to go with it. All currencies were accepted – Russian, Chinese, Indian, American or Sterling. Checking on-line recently, I discovered via Wiki-Voyage that 'the *Smuggler's Bazaar* has since been moved to Dara Khel, and 'the Landi Kotal bazaar is now just a pale shadow of its previous infamy'.

Still on the subject of culture and politics: I have toured in East and West Africa, and was invited back to the Ethiopian capital of Addis Ababa to advise on possible technical improvements to their National Theatre. I arrived at the same time as planeloads of Cuban soldiers. They were there to support the Mengistu communist coup. One morning I got a phone call from the British Council telling me not to leave the hotel: I had heard gun-shots outside, and could see roadblocks each end of the main street. The following morning it was quiet: the Theatre Director picked me up in his car and, on the way to the theatre, I tried to get his thoughts about what it was really like living and working under these conditions. He simply lifted up a map by the gear lever to reveal a loaded pistol. 'If they stop me, I'll try to take at least one of them with me'.

During fit-ups in India and Africa I would often join the theatre technicians on their tea-breaks – sometimes squatting at the side of the road drinking tea from an old baked bean tin. Perhaps this helped to build up an immunity: I only had one serious bout of tummy-trouble in all my tours – but health was a regular concern for the more-cautious actors.

During an African tour (not one of mine) of *Romeo and Juliet*, Romeo had just arrived in the tomb to discover the apparently-dead Juliet when his stomach started to heave: he rushed outside to throw-up in the bushes. Left alone, Juliet - a young Judi Dench - decided she couldn't just lie there. She woke up, looked around the empty stage, and, playing for time, said 'where's Romeo?' A voice from the audience said 'He think you dead. He gone looking for another woman'.

On one Indian tour the actors refused to hire rickshaws because 'It's immoral to expect a fellow-man to pull you around the streets' and, anyway, 'do you know the life expectancy of a rickshaw-wallah?' I explained that it was his business, his profession. They were actors: he was a rickshaw-wallah. He rented the rickshaw: without customers he couldn't pay the rent for the rickshaw; he couldn't pay the rent for his home, and his family might not eat that night. There was a lot a chat in the dressing room but, by the end of the performance they had solved the moral dilemma. They hired rickshaws, which they pulled back to the hotel themselves with the rickshaw-wallahs sitting in the back.

My *meanderings* occasionally took me to Scandinavia. On one occasion I was the sole British representative at a Dance Theatre Festival in Finland; a wonderful experience. Most of the participants were 'Nordic' but included the dazzling Christina Hoyos heading her company of Spanish dancers and musicians. That was a great night, with several *encores* at the end: even then we wouldn't let them go, encouraging them back for yet another bow. They drifted on, looking uncertain, unrehearsed, almost embarrassed – before going into the best routine of the night, with the musicians joining in the dancing, and with fully-plotted lighting cues. Unrehearsed? Huh!

I do thrill to that kind of professionalism. I remember, early on, seeing Ken Dodd at his brilliant best (he was a sad figure towards the end; all energy gone). He was telling one of his longer stories when his trio suddenly started to play, quietly but obviously. I thought it was odd up to the point where he finished the story at exactly the same moment as they finished the introduction, and they segued perfectly together into one of his songs. So professional. That moment was tucked away in a corner of my brain for future reference.

On my way home from the Nordic Dance Theatre Festival I enjoyed my first visit to the impressive Tivoli Gardens in Denmark where top-quality international live entertainment plays such a key role, and was reminded of the time the Old Vic took Tyrone Guthrie's production of *Hamlet* to Elsinore Castle, with Olivier as the Prince.

The castle was open to the public all day, so they had to rehearse at night. The Danish Royal Family were already on their way to the opening performance when the heavens opened, and everything had to be hastily moved into the ballroom of the hotel – and performed (with little rehearsal time) in the round. Newspaper critics helped to re-arrange the 850 seats. It proved a *Hamlet of more than ordinary vitality*, strengthening Guthrie's conviction that the proscenium arch is unsatisfactory for Shakespeare. That audience, he thought, related to the play in a more logical, satisfactory and effective way than can ever be achieved in an orthodox theatre. It was probably that night which decided his future involvement in the 1953 Stratford Shakespearean Festival in Ontario, Canada, and all that followed. Full details of that and much else in one of *the* classic theatre autobiographies, Tyrone Guthrie's *A Life In The Theatre*.

In this theatrical tour of the world I haven't mentioned America, so let's end this chapter with a Jack Benny story about Fanny Brice.

A long time ago an American Vaudeville duo, youngsters Jesse Block and Eva Sully, were in the number four slot on a variety bill at the Chicago Theatre.

Top of the bill was Fanny Brice, the great Jewish comedienne and singer: she liked their act, and took the youngsters to a party at the home of the gangster Al Capone. The party was in Fanny's honour, and afterwards they all went on to a nightclub, the College Inn, and they had a great time.

Many years later, Fanny Brice was in a nursing home. Jesse and Eva were in the area so called in to see her, but her memory was going and she couldn't remember them; couldn't even remember working with them.

'We played the Chicago Theatre together'.

'Couldn't have: I never played the Chicago Theatre'.

'Sure you did' said Jesse. 'And one night after the show you took us to a party at Al Capone's house'.

'Al Capone, huh'. She shook her head. 'Nah, I was never in Al Capone's house'.

'And after they party we all went on to the College Inn, had a great time'.

Fanny laughed. 'Nah, that never happened. Sorry'.

'It did, Fanny, believe me, it did. You were top of the bill. They paid you seventy-five hundred for the week'.

'Seventy-five hundred? Seventy-five hundred? Nah, you don't remember anything. I got eighty-five hundred'!

CHAPTER TWENTY
NOTTINGHAM NIGHTS

In 1968 I had the honour and pleasure of welcoming Dame Sybil Thorndike to Nottingham for a poetry recital at the last of the Playhouse annual Arts Festivals (replaced later by the first city-wide official Nottingham Festival). The great lady was by then 86 years old and much venerated, and we made a special effort: painted the dressing room, fitted a carpet, arranged for flowers, and a car to collect her from the station.

My four stage hands at Nottingham had been recruited from the Job Centre, put out of work because of the slump in the mining industry. They had no theatre experience and had never heard of Dame Sybil Thorndike. They couldn't understand why we were making all this fuss over some ageing actress and were standing around with beer-bottles in unwashed hands when she arrived. She put down her bags and went straight across to them; shook the unwashed hands, asked them their names (which she remembered at the end of the recital), and chatted to them for twenty minutes about their families, life in Nottingham, the problems of the mining industry. Committed Christian, committed Socialist, she really cared about people and about causes. Those four lads stood, spell-bound, through a poetry recital and at the end were queueing up outside her dressing room to carry her bags and her flowers, and waving their goodbyes as the car pulled away.

Bernard Shaw once auditioned Sybil for a touring production of *Candida*, but she was 'so young, so innocent. I told her to get married, have children, have a decade of housework, and then she would know what *Candida* was all about'. After years of procrastination on the subject of Saint Joan – 'I couldn't find a way into it' – he saw Sybil in a production of Shelley's verse play *The Cenci* and 'knew that at last I had found my Joan: from that moment the words poured forth in torrents, I could scarcely get them down on paper quickly enough'. In the intervening years Sybil had married Lewis Casson, had four children, and had a decade of housekeeping. Shaw invited Sybil and  Lewis Casson to his home at Ayot St Lawrence where, of course, he read the entire play to them. 'Read it beautifully' she said. 'He ought to have been an actor really. From the moment he started we couldn't move. It was the most amazing experience. And when he got to the epilogue, Lewis and I were both in tears'.

A young John Gielgud was at the first night of *St Joan* at the New Theatre in March 1924, and described Sybil Thorndike as 'the best-loved English actress since Ellen Terry'. James Agate wrote of the play 'There is a faintly jovial, quasi-satirical, and wholly unnecessary epilogue, conceived in a vein of lesser exaltation. Mr Shaw excuses this on the ground that without it the play could be *only a sensational tale of a girl who was burnt*. The production was beyond any praise of mine. The scenery, designed by Mr Charles Ricketts, was neither frankly representational nor uncompromisingly expressionistic, but a happy blend of the two. The dresses made a kind of music in the air, and at the end Joan was allowed to stand for a moment in all that ecstasy of tinsel and blue in which French image-makers enshrine her memory. As Joan, Miss Thorndike had three admirable moments: when she said 'they do'; when she listened in the Ambulatory to the pronouncement of desertion to come, and when she listened to the recantation. Her Joan was excellent; boyish, brusque, inspired, exalted, manner-less, tactless and obviously (after she had served her turn) a nuisance to everybody. Miss Thorndike did nobly'.

I never saw Dame Sybil's *St Joan*, although I did see her as Teresa of Avila at the Vaudeville Theatre in late 1961. The production received what she called *the familiar audience/critic split*. 'Our first night was a riot – yells and bravos and curtain after curtain, but the reviews were a great disappointment' and the production closed after six weeks.

I had moved to Nottingham Playhouse at the invitation of Stuart Burge and George Rowbottom. Stuart had directed a Christopher Fry premiere *Curtmantle* at the Aldwych during my time at the RSC; George had been  stage manager on Blitz!, and Administrator at the National Theatre during my year at the Old Vic.

They had scheduled a quite extraordinary repertoire for their first year at Nottingham: it included Ben Jonson's *The Alchemist*; Shaw's *Widower's Houses*; Singe's *Playboy of the Western World;* John Osborne's *The Entertainer*; Brecht's *Arturo Ui*; Shakespeare's *Macbeth*; a rarely-performed Farquhar, *Love and a Bottle*; and two world premieres – *The Ruling Class* by Peter Barnes, and Fry's *A Yard of Sun*. One of the many joys of that first season was the production of *King Lear* offering the chance to work with both Jonathan Miller (director) and Michael Hordern (a superb Lear). Rehearsals were fascinating not least because Jonathan, as a qualified doctor, was able to diagnose the exact medical condition of Lear from the symptoms provided within Shakespeare's text. I first met up with Michael Hordern at the RSC when he coped wonderfully with Ulysses' great speech in *Troilus and Cressida*. Our last meeting was in Oxford Street: the by-then-Sir Michael, about eighty years old, saw me from the other side of the road and wove his way through the busy traffic just to say hello. A lovely man. I was abroad when Michael played the doddery old waiter in Shaw's *You Never Can Tell*. I'm sorry to have missed that; it sounds like perfect casting.

I've never had a particular urge (or an opportunity) to direct Shakespeare, although I do have a great many thoughts about a possible *King Lear*, most of them relating to the ages of the characters. It is nonsense to say, as one of our leading theatrical knights recently did, that 78 is the right age to play Lear (and, yes, I know that the original King Leir ruled for over sixty years). Shakespeare's Lear has three daughters: one about to be married; the other two presumably recently-married since there are, so far, no children – so probably not the children of a 78-year-old.

The first grandson to be born might have a strong claim to the throne – perhaps the reason why both sisters are lusting after the bastard Edmund, each of them equally desperate to bear the heir which their husbands have not so far provided. I am convinced that this is a play for a younger, hot-blooded cast.

A few days prior to his death Shakespeare was visited by Ben Jonson, aged 46 and Michael Drayton aged 53: in the play Kent claims to 'have years on my back forty-eight'. This line sometimes evokes laughter but we should remember that Shakespeare died at 52, having fathered three children; Susanna (married with a young daughter), Judith pregnant before her marriage, and a favourite son Hamnet lost to the plague.

The Fool's age is no longer governed by the probable doubling of the part with that of Cordelia, and therefore played by a boy. Jonathan Miller cast mature Frank Middlemass as Hordern's Fool: a wonderful double act – and that opens up possibilities for the Fool in other scenes – the opening scene, for instance, when he does not appear because (one assumes) he was already on stage playing Cordelia. He would also be a bonus at the end, adding even more pathos to Lear's death. 'And my poor Fool is dead' was clearly a late addition to the script to cover the fact that with Cordelia's body on the stage the Fool was *unavailable*.

Stuart had programmed John Osborne's musical play *The Entertainer* but was having trouble casting the title role. Prior to my arrival in Nottingham I had been 'around the world' stage managing Max Adrian's one-man-show as GBS. In Australia, we had lunched with Denis Quilley in Sydney's Quantas Hotel, *where the big stars stay*. Denis had co-starred with Max in *Airs on a Shoestring* at the Royal Court. Max had played Pangloss in the original Broadway production of Bernstein's *Candide*: Denis had starred in the title role of Candide in London -

the first West End musical I saw after my demob from the RAF - so we had *Candide* in common to kick-start the conversation.

What I didn't appreciate at that time was that Denis had been a 'student' under Michel Saint-Denis at the London Theatre Studio. Denis had arrived in Australia with a tour of *Robert and Elizabeth*, and stayed on to play the leading role of Inspector Hallam in what proved to be a successful, long-running TV series *Contrabandits* which he described as '*Z-cars by Sydney Bridge*'. With the series drawing towards a conclusion Denis was planning to return to the UK. I suggested him to Stuart as a possible Archie Rice: Stuart remembered him as *a skinny young singing actor* but I was able to confirm that he had matured and filled out. We practically met him at the airport: he accepted, joined us in Nottingham, and was superb in the role. Michael Blakemore saw *The Entertainer* one evening, and told Denis he ought to be at the National Theatre. 'My God, I'd love that' said Denis. Blakemore talked to Olivier, and within months they were both at the National Theatre, Michael as Associate Director, and Denis in a wide range of leading roles – including co-starring with Olivier in *Long Day's Journey into Night*. He worked regularly at the National during the rest of his life: *there was a vacant slot for a man of my age and weight in the upper-middle of the company, and I just happened to fit it*. He went on to star in two major West End musicals, *Sweeney Todd* and *La Cage Aux Folles*. I'm happy to think that I might have played a very tiny part in the success story of this friendly, talented, hard-working guy. In that same season I also engaged a young, Leicester-born drama student as Acting ASM. His name was Michael Kitchen. I wonder what happened to him.

After two busy years as Repertoire Manager I was head-hunted to help set up the first of the city-wide Nottingham Festivals in 1969. Hopes were high: *the biggest, the most stupendous* according to the Nottingham Post, *it will rival Edinburgh*. The budget was £25,000 – good for the time, but hardly of Edinburgh proportions. Director Richard Gregson-Williams was, like so many Festival directors, essentially a 'music man', and I found myself increasingly involved in the organisation of the popular outdoor events in Wollaton Park.

There, the final evening included a Jousting Tournament, and a firework display attended by 50,000 people. I had a feeling that the jousting event might be interesting when I heard that one of the film stuntmen involved had phoned his opponent to talk tactics and was told 'Tactics be damned; I'm going to knock thee off tha bloody 'orse'. We also ran a daily programme in the Old Market Square (*right*).

I had a lovely flat in The Park, a quiet Victorian residential area just behind the Castle, and was reluctant to move. Happily, with the Festival, the two theatres (Playhouse and Theatre Royal), and my tours with Sadlers Wells Ballet, there was plenty of freelance work available. I toured with the Playhouse TIE company (we gave Sandi Toksvig her first acting job), and stage managed a couple of pantomimes at the Theatre Royal.

Productions during this period included *Black Comedy* with students at Oakham School, and the amateur premiere of Ben Travers' last play *The Bed Before Yesterday* at the charming little Robin Hood Theatre in Averham, just north of Nottingham, long associated with Donald Wolfit. Ben Travers sent a telegram: *Congratulations. The amateur premiere of my latest play: another milestone in my long career.*

The old (long-closed) Empire Theatre adjacent to the Theatre Royal was being demolished to make way for the new Concert Hall by the time I eventually, and reluctantly, gave up my flat and moved on. Happily, my Nottingham residency had a 'big finish'. Someone, probably the Playhouse Head of Design Patrick Robertson who had designed *Waiting for Godot* at the Bristol Old Vic during my National Service days, relayed a message to Stuart Burge that Mr O'Toole 'might be interested in doing the play again for a 'short run' in a quality provincial playhouse'. The production was scheduled: I was engaged as CSM, and the cast was O'Toole as Vladimir; Donal McCann as Estragon; Niall Toibin as Pozzo and Frank Middlemass as Lucky. We rehearsed in London, and arrived in Nottingham to discover that the entire three-week run was Sold Out.

According to the programme the Director was Frederick Monoyer, a hat which O'Toole occasionally wore whenever he directed himself in a production. I can't guarantee this, but I don't think Mr Monoyer ever directed anything which did not star Mr O'Toole. Whichever of them was responsible, he did an excellent job, and the reviews were overwhelmingly good. Not for the first time at a Samuel Beckett production Harold Hobson went 'over the top': *for the length of its run this production makes Nottingham Playhouse the theatrical capital of England.*

Peter's drinking seemed to be under control, and he agreed to be Guest of Honour at the Playhouse Supporter's Club annual Dinner and Dance on the second Sunday. Obviously the dinner was a sell-out, with the ladies all freshly coiffed and ready to meet – perhaps even dance with - Lawrence of Arabia. Dinner was finished and cleared away, but no sign of their Guest. The dancing started, and indeed was almost over when our rather-the-worse-for-wear Vladimir wove his way into the hall and onto the platform having, we learnt, spent the evening with the Theatre Royal pantomime company in a local hostelry.

There was little left for him to do except draw the raffle, and he desperately tried to focus on the stationary ticket as he slowly swayed past it, first one way, then the other. Finally success: 'Blue ticket forty-two'. A long pause. No claimants. The glazed eyes grew a little tighter, the voice a little tetchier. 'Blue ticket forty-two'. The fixed smile slowly disappeared as the evening drew towards its apparently inevitable conclusion. 'Oh fuck 'em' he said, give us another ticket'.

 In January 1989, as Manager of the Adam Smith Theatre in Kirkcaldy, I was celebrating the thirtieth anniversary of my first theatre appointment. Peter sent me a card saying 'May you manage another thirty years'. In January of this year, I did. How I wish he could have been around to join in the celebrations.

A great character; a great talent: greatly missed.

CHAPTER TWENTY-ONE
WRITING FOR THE THEATRE

'The legibly-written novel exists as the sole intermediary between the creative and the perceptive brain. The slowness of its processes differentiates the typical novel from the typical play. But the drama, before it can make its proper appeal at all, must be run through a highly complex piece of mechanism known as the theatre, the precise conditions of which are, to most, a fascinating mystery. As fiction is the art of gradual development, the drama may be called the art of crises. The dramatist deals in rapid and startling changes which may be the outcome of long slow processes, but which actually occur in very brief spaces of time'.

That was written by **William Archer** in a 1912 book titled *Play-Making, a Manual of Craftsmanship* which remains a useful starting point for any potential playwright even though it begins with the stark warning 'There are no rules for writing a play: the quest for such rules is apt to result in either pedantry or quackery'. As an example he offers the 'rule' that would-be playwrights should not let their characters narrate their circumstances or expound their motives in speeches addressed either directly to the audience, or to themselves - which would appear to rule out Richard the Third's 'Now is the winter of our discontent' and Hamlet's 'Oh, what a rogue and peasant slave am I'. We are indeed fortunate that Shakespeare didn't follow rules.

Another 'rule' oft-quoted in my early theatre days was that *Conflict is the essence of drama*. Perhaps, accepts Archer, although probably not extended over two or three acts, and he offers a more subtle variation *No obstacle, no drama* as having a certain practical usefulness. He suggests *crisis* rather than *conflict*. 'A play is a more-or-less developing crisis in circumstance or destiny, and a dramatic scene is a crisis within a crisis, clearly furthering the ultimate event'.

J B Priestley in *The Art of the Dramatist* also differentiates clearly between plays and books. 'A dramatist writes for the theatre. A man who writes to be read and not to be performed is not a dramatist. The poet or novelist turns away from drama; he looks inward not outward; he is introverted, not extroverted; his mind explores itself, not palaces, senates, markets and taverns. The dramatist keeps in mind not the printer but a company of actors, not book-readers but play-goers. He is as closely tied to the theatre as a chef is to the kitchen, with the ultimate objective, even though he cannot achieve it by himself, of the creation of *a dramatic experience*'.

Harley Granville-Barker shied at the very phrase *the principles of dramatic art*. Urging the formulation of the principles of playwriting is *a mischievous thing*, he thought.

The dramatist's task differs from that of the novelist: each wants to tell a story; the novelist can write a hundred thousand words while the dramatist must be content with twenty thousand or so. The would-be dramatist is encouraged to think that he has only to pin up a set of rules over his desk and follow them like a recipe and all will be well. But this is how puddings are made; not plays; not good plays, certainly – nor the best puddings for that matter. Even Aristotle was against rules, preferring '*you had better*' to '*you must*'.

Actor **Sir Cedric Hardwicke** in one of the best theatre biographies I have ever read, *A Victorian in Orbit*, implied that Pinero, Sardou and Wilde prospered as makers of plays because they understood that a play is not to be written like a novel, but *wrought* as a wheelwright makes a wheel. 'The theatre, the most explicit of the arts and therefore the most conservative, demands ideas and truths in their most abstracted form – poetic truths. I wish more playwrights would turn their attentions to fiction. Either that or start writing plays that let in the actor so that he, in turn, can let in the audience. The audience is an essential character in every good play, for without its help and sympathy no play can succeed'. Hardwicke thought that the only two commercial writers to have survived in the history of the drama were Shaw, the man of mind, and Shakespeare, man of heart and full of passion. 'Without them, actors might well amount to little more than a bunch of clowns'.

So – where to start? Peter Gill suggests with **Tom Robertson** (1829-1871) the playwright who, according to John Russell Taylor, was the first to 'adopt a light intimate style of short speeches, each one taking up the thread of what has gone before in an easy, natural-seeming way. The characters seem to be listening to, and answering each other for the audience's benefit, rather than speaking to the audience. In his most-famous play *Caste* the conversation developed *almost to the exclusion of plot*, requiring the actors to play as an ensemble rather than as individuals waiting to deliver their big speeches'.

Taylor called Robertson *a new voice in the theatre and a whole new approach to the business of drama*, but did accept that Robertson was influenced by similar developments in France, and particularly by the writings of Eugène Scribe.

With style established, we might return to **William Archer**: 'One thing we may say with tolerable confidence – the play will be of small account as a work of art unless 'character' enters at a very early point in the development. And characters capable of unexpected developments, *or less characters they*. No outside force should appear to control the free rhythm of the action: if it does then the writer may be pretty sure that it is a piece of mechanism he is putting together, not a drama with flesh and blood in it'.

C K Munro: 'It is quite possible to suspend tension for a considerable time with a set of characters able to amuse or charm or arouse sympathy. However, the playwright's first task is the modest one of keeping the audience in their seats until the end of the play, so he must have an aim, a goal which in the end is gained or lost. Generally speaking, the thing which binds people to the seats in a theatre is suspense, and its progressive satisfaction.

André Obey, playwright for *Compagnie des Quinze*, didn't bother with any idea of a thesis, of symbolism, or of pointing a moral: 'I thought of the stage, and that was enough. My theory is that a play is a *thing of the theatre*, strictly and yet freely-invented for the stage, composed and developed on the stage, subjected to the stage to such an extent that the life, the reality and the rhythm arrive before the words. The play exists in my imagination before it is written down; the pattern of action on the stage, the sequence of events, form a tangible structure in my mind; the moods and emotions of the characters are there before the text is put on paper'.

Or, like me, you can follow **Harley Granville-Barker**'s advice: Get yourself pens and paper and a large waste-paper basket.

I have quoted **Tom Stoppard** elsewhere: 'A writer is not in control; he writes what he has to write'. For a playwright things are more complicated: you must first of all be confident that whatever it is you *have to write* will only work as a play, perhaps even more specifically as a stage play, a radio play or a screen-play. **C K Munro** again: 'The thing a play is really about can essentially never be said: if it could, there would be no need to make a play about it'. One recalls Isadora Duncan: 'No, I can't explain the dance to you; if I could say it, *I wouldn't have to dance it'*.

Ashley Dukes advised 'Start with a good title: that is useful because of its power of suggestion'. He recalled marching in 1915 as a soldier past some roadside alehouse called *The Man with a Load of Mischief*. The sign immediately suggested *a comedy* and 'dialogue began to run through my head'. During the summer of 1924 the finished script was shown to several London producing managers all of whom said there was not a penny in it; which opinion he entirely shared. In June 1925 it was acquired by Frederick Harrison for the Haymarket and Dukes suddenly found himself with an income of close on a thousand pounds a month, more than he would normally require in a year.

Thus it is that plays contrive to get themselves written and produced, sometimes after maturing through years of personal experience and emotional impulse to which a technical understanding of the writer's craft is more or less unconsciously added.

John Whiting in a 1961 Encore interview:
Thomas Mann said 'Writing is more difficult for writers than for other people'.

'I construct my plays on a sort of thematic basis, almost a subconscious thing, and it never seemed frightfully important to me that an audience should recognise it. I have to find some way of putting the wretched stuff down on paper and this just happens to be my method. Everybody has different methods.

With actors there's the danger of over-investigation: that's their method. My method is to work on a sort of musical shape'. (Gielgud said that Shaw asked them to treat the script for *Arms and the Man* as a musical score).

'There is an accumulation of ideas within the comparatively short time you spend in the theatre: many people will miss some points, but analysis in performance is exactly like over-criticism of music. *The subscription of the flute* at a certain bar is not important but it is often picked out. To make it a play, somebody's got to say something, and therefore one has to find the significant points in it, and a shape. It's the *total effect* which matters'.

I have some sympathy with John Whiting's view about *the subscription of the flute at a certain* bar. Enjoyment of performances in both theatre and concert hall has occasionally been diminished for me by *too much attention to detail* weakening the *total effect* – sometimes even by master-craftsmen such as Simon Rattle or Trevor Nunn. Or even Toscanini. This is by James Agate, published on 9.5.1939: 'Heard Toscanini last night for the first time. Coriolan Overture, the Fourth Symphony, and the Eroica. This was drilled music. *I heard things in the score for the first time,* but was reminded of when I took my long-distance spectacles into the country, saw every leaf distinctly, and lost all sense of atmosphere! What I heard last night was a *map* of the music, or Beethoven anatomised. Personally I like my Beethoven to be more human, less tidy, a little more sprawling, more beer- and tobacco-stained'.

I mentioned **Trevor Nunn:** he wanted playwrights to be more ambitious. 'Tony Kushner (who wrote *Angels in America*) has exhilarating ambition, and we yearn for more. When it happens we recognise it as the real thing, but it's also a rare thing. It's partly economic; writers are advised *don't invent more than five characters because your play will never get on; don't invent too many scenic requirements because your main chance of a staging is in a room above a pub'.*

Robert Bolt, in another Encore interview: 'It's a familiar phenomenon at university – thinking oneself a writer, without actually writing anything. Then, in my first job, teaching at the village school, the headmistress said 'Do a Nativity Play' and handed me a great batch of those little plays that are published for children to read. They were either unspeakably dull or unspeakably mawkish so I started to write one myself. Literally within about five lines of dialogue the penny dropped, and I thought 'This is what I want to do. It was an extraordinary sensation. It excited me. As soon as I had finished the Nativity Play I wrote a play for radio and it was accepted. I was a playwright!' *Robert Bolt's tambourine moment?*

'Before I start I must have the general structure: I must know where the play is going to end – I don't just follow my nose. And I must know roughly how that beginning is going to get to that end. Then each scene must have a beginning, a middle and an end. My influences are mostly poetic and all roads end at Shakespeare. Brecht is the writer I would most wish to resemble: he didn't always manage the balance between passion and intellect, but theatrically he was right – particularly what he said about language, *a noble, dignified prose architecture is the primary alienation effect.* I wrote with subtlety rather than complexity. And wrote sufficient big parts for various knights and dames to earn me an honest living".

Kenneth Tynan said of Bolt's script for *A Man for All Seasons* that there were 'some muscular pieces of period prose'. An amused Robert Bolt thought that the quote would have pleased Sir Thomas More – the original writer of those particular 'muscular pieces'.

Mr **G Bernard Shaw**'s route to becoming *Britain's second-greatest playwright* started badly. He arrived in England in early 1876, aged twenty, to join his mother and sister Lucy: together they went immediately to Ventnor on the Isle of Wight for the funeral of his elder sister Agnes who had died of phthisis.

Back in London, he wrote 'careful music criticism, carefully phrased' for *The Hornet*, but in the name of George John Vandaleur Lee, his mother's former *singing teacher* who was contracted for the work but was himself *no writer*. A Shavian style developed, the editor smelt a rat, and Lee's contract was ended.

In 1879 Shaw began work on a novel, his first attempt at a 'big book'. It was mainly autobiographical, and handwritten since he could not afford a typewriter.

He *condemned himself* to five pages a day: if the fifth page ended in the middle of a sentence 'I did not finish it until the next day'. The novel's title was *Immaturity* and, along with its two successors, it was turned down by *every publisher in Great Britain and America*.

Hoping for some work as a critic he wrote to the editor of the *Pall Mall Gazette*, John Morley, who replied that in his opinion Shaw would do well to get out of journalism. 'In truth' Shaw commented, 'I was hardly in it'.

The Shaws (mother and son: sister Lucy was on tour with an opera company) moved to Fitzroy Street, close to the British Museum where the magnificent Reading Room provided GBS with 'office space' for the next eight years. The local restaurants fed his newly acquired vegetarianism, and an attack of smallpox left him with a scar on his right cheek encouraging him to grow the big red bushy beard. His poverty and social awkwardness made him 'a complete outsider' – outside of literary and social life, and not yet in politics - although that was about to change. The publication in serial form of his latest novel *The Unsocial Socialist* brought him no money, but did bring him to the attention of William Morris with whom Shaw shared political platforms on Sundays. It also brought him an offer of a post on the political staff of *The Star* under the editorship of the liberal T P O'Connor. Unlike O'Connor, Shaw had studied Karl Marx in his British Museum *office*, so his socialist articles did not sit easily on the liberal editor's pages: rather than sack him, they moved him to the arts section as a music critic.

All of *The Star* critics wrote under pseudonyms, and Shaw chose for himself the name Corno di Bassetto hoping to suggest an Italian nobleman although it is, in fact, the name of a 'vulgar musical instrument known in English as the basset horn'. He couldn't deny that Bassetto was also occasionally vulgar but thought that didn't matter so long as he made people laugh. *I was merely playing the clown.*

His increasing interest in politics took him to the Zetetical Debating Society where he attempted his first speech 'making a complete and utter fool of myself'. Reading their first pamphlet *Why are the Many Poor?* led him to the Fabian Society, which he joined in 1884, being elected to the committee a year later. He would serve on that committee for twenty-six years.

Music criticism led to theatre criticism, to a friendship with William Archer and their shared admiration for the plays of Ibsen. Together they wrote the first two acts of a play provisionally titled *Rhinegold*. Later, even more under the influence of Ibsen, and remembering his experiences collecting slum rentals in Dublin, Shaw rewrote the two acts, added a third, and the result was *Widower's Houses*, produced by J T Grein's Independent Theatre Company for just two performances on the 9th and 13th December 1892. It made him instantly *infamous, blasted by a whirlwind of abuse* but that didn't concern him too much: 'All the little tricks I had planned worked perfectly' he said, 'and convinced me that I was a born master of the theatre'.

Some men are born playwrights: Harley Granville-Barker wrote his first play (with Herbert Thomas) when he was only eighteen, and his second a year later. Some men achieve playwriting: witness G B Shaw above, who was twice that age at the time of *Widower's Houses,* and 38 before he had a first success with *Arms and the Man.* I had playwriting 'thrust upon me'. I had already accepted a post as General Manager of Kirkcaldy's Adam Smith Theatre when they pointed out that the contract covered responsibility for the writing, production and direction of the annual pantomime.

By then I had already directed three Gilbert & Sullivan light operas and a 'thrust stage' version of Chekhov's *Three Sisters* in Scotland, and I'd worked on professional pantomimes – backstage at the Palladium, stage managing at Nottingham's Theatre Royal, and directing an amateur *Aladdin* in Bahrain, so the production and directing side didn't concern me too much. But 'writing'? And in such a 'stylised' form? Alarm bells rang.

Fortunately I took up the post in October by which time my predecessor Chris Potter had written most of the book for *Jack and the Beanstalk*, cast most of the performers, and ordered most of the scenery. Chris and I shared a love of musicals so I knew his song selection would be appropriate: unfortunately he'd booked the musicians from an agency, and pantomime proved rather too strenuous for the elderly musical director they sent us. Apart from that it worked pretty well – and I still had almost a year to plan my first script.

In my second Palladium panto Harry Secombe, playing Humpty Dumpty, sang a Welsh folk song *David of the White Rock*. In Welsh. Why? Well, my guess was that it was his latest recording: they probably hoped that by singing it in the pantomime they would sell more copies of the record. Anyway, a Welsh folk song in the middle of *Humpty Dumpty* seemed totally out of place to me, and I made a mental note that when (not if, you notice), *when* I directed my first pantomime all the songs and dances would be as relevant to the plot as in any of the best musicals. I was therefore delighted to read Mary Brennan's review in the *Glasgow Herald* 'I was very much taken with the way director Brian Freeland and choreographer Jane Harrod make the various dance sequences fit in with the story. In other panto villages the streets are hoaching with grinning peasants. Here a chorus of merry milkmaids pursue a recalcitrant cow while in a later scene a group of the Giant's prisoners droop and pine in chains. This kind of inventiveness helps refresh traditions and makes Kirkcaldy's *Jack and the Beanstalk* a lively and entertaining show'.

Once *Jack* had opened I travelled around Scotland seeing all the possibly-available pantomime performers. Chris Potter had usually engaged London-based artistes, but the plot I had in mind for my first solo script would require an obviously-Scottish company. Seeing them all working, especially in panto, would make casting easier, and it would greatly ease my script problems if I could write for specific performers. I had a quiet word in the theatre bars afterwards with a few of the more-likely candidates; two of my 'principals' were immediately 'pencilled-in'. I found folk/ jazz singer Alastair McDonald playing a very butch Dame in Glasgow, and magician/compere John Shearer at the MacRobert Centre in Stirling doing both panto and children's shows. A lovely man, John, sadly no longer with us, and I miss those happy evenings spent with John and Eleanor at their family home in Dollar. Over on the west coast I noticed a young performer with a pleasant stage personality and an ill-fitting costume: two years later Micky McPherson was headlining as our Robinson Crusoe.

My first *Humpty Dumpty* would be very different version to Harry Secombe's: I wanted Humpty to come out of the egg as a stranger in a foreign country, not understanding the language, a total alien. I now had a Scottish cast – but where would I find an 'alien'? On television, as it turned out, narrowly nudged into second place in the finals of *New Faces*. A natural clown, visually hilarious, and with a voice that made him an 'alien' even in his native London. Yes, Joe Pasquale. He took a bit of convincing: this would be only his second pantomime, and his first appearance in Scotland.

To 'test the water' I scheduled three nights of variety, with Joe topping the bill: his support acts were all Scottish contestants from his series of *New Faces* (each heat had participants from the various English regions and from Wales and Scotland). At the end of Joe's spot on the Saturday evening the Compere asked the audience if they would like to see him back as star of the next Kirkcaldy panto, and their enthusiasm was so obvious that Joe was won over.

'Humpty Dumpty is a good egg' wrote reporter Allan Crow in the Fife Free Press: his clever way with words eventually saw him promoted to editor. 'Joe Pasquale shines in the starring role thanks to his madcap features and zany presentation. He really is a few pine needles short of a Christmas tree, but comes across as the kids' best friend – and gets up to everything youngsters shouldn't'. With wonderful support, especially from Micky McPherson's eager-but-simple Prince Simon, any short-comings in my first-ever script were happily glossed-over.

The musical side of pantomime was as important to me as the comedy or the spectacle and, at a time when most Scottish provincial pantomimes were making do with electric piano and drums, I always engaged four musicians. This meant that we had to use the orchestra pit, opening up a black hole between performers and audience. For my final panto I was determined to bring everything closer to the audience by covering over the orchestra pit: this involved writing, designing and directing a show which could incorporate an on-stage band. The subject would be *Robinson Crusoe*, but not in the traditional Defoe version. The original 'Crusoe', Alexander Selkirk, was a Fife man, born in the fishing village of Lower Largo just seven miles north of Kirkcaldy, and I planned to bring his story 'home'. We set the opening scenes in Lower Largo following a prologue set in the grounds of a modern holiday hotel on a once-desert island, with guests on sun-loungers – and a quartet of musicians playing in a down-stage corner. The hotel manager (versatile actor John Adam Baker, who would reappear as an unexpectedly-intellectual Man Friday) explains to the guests that the evening's entertainment will tell the story of the first white man to arrive in the islands, one Robinson Crusoe. The hotel front-cloth disappears: we are in Lower Largo – and the on-stage band is still there, established and accepted.

Dame that Christmas was Fife-born, London-based 'drag act' Nicky Young. He had seen *Humpty Dumpty* the previous year, and told me it 'looked so far away' seen across the pit.

He had his doubts about whether the on-stage band would work or not, but wholly endorsed the closer relationship with the audience. Micky McPherson was Robinson Crusoe, addressed throughout as Robbie. Replacing the traditional Prince was Robbie's brother Rickie, short for Enrico Crusoe (the name made *me* laugh, but I'm old enough to remember the opera singer Enrico Caruso). The Dame character was, of course, their mother Mrs Crusoe. We were fortunate to get a really hissable baddie, Derek Lord from Scottish Television's *Take the High Road* as the Laird o' Lundy.

In September 1704 Alexander Selkirk had been put ashore on the island of Juan Fernando after a disagreement with his captain over the seaworthiness of their ship. He was alone on that island for over four years with only feral goats for company (no, there was no Man Friday). The goats provided him with meat, milk and hides for clothing. I wanted to find some way to demonstrate this *loneliness* within a pantomime, and asked circus owner Tommy Chipperfield whether he had any trained goats we could borrow. He smiled politely as people do with simpletons, and explained gently that you cannot 'train' goats. A dog, a horse or an elephant is capable of learning a complete routine, and would perform perfectly even without the trainer in the ring, but goats do not have that facility. What they can do, however, what they love to do, is

climb. Put a box or a barrel in front of them and they will jump on it. He used goats occasionally in public shows: the trainer simply built up ever-higher levels of planks and boxes, and encouraged the goats to do exactly what they would have done anyway. This was perfect: Crusoe was on a desert island: driftwood could logically be scattered around the stage, so we had a deal. Chipperfield's trainer spent a day with Micky McPherson to show him the ropes, and then drove off. He had lost a winter's feed bill: we had gained three pygmy goats.

They were quite unpredictable, but the audiences loved them and they proved the real 'stars' of the show – twice daily. All through this *period of loneliness* the band remained on stage, sharing the audience's enjoyment of the goats' unpredictability, and reminding me of another piece of advice from **C K Munro**: The art of the theatre is like conjuring: you direct the attention of the audience to the most important thing happening at any moment by controlling movement and grouping on stage; by inflection, by gesture or pause. The 'art' is to draw to the audiences notice to the things which the dramatist regards as crucial'.

I recommend all aspiring playwrights to read **Moss Hart**'s memoir *Act One*, recording the writing, and rewriting, and rewriting and yet more rewriting of his first hit *Once in a Lifetime*. The laughs were drying up half-way through the show, and they were constantly adding more jokes, more sets, more props, all without success.

A few days before the Broadway opening Moss Hart and the manager, Sam Harris, were drowning their sorrows ahead of a certain flop when Harris said "'I wish it weren't such a noisy play, kid.'
'What do you mean, a noisy play?'
'Just think about it. Except for those two minutes at the beginning of the first act there isn't another spot in this whole play where two people sit down and talk quietly to each other. It tires an audience out. That stage is so damn full of actors and scenery and costumes and props they never get a chance to catch their breath and listen. It's a noisy play, kid'.

Overnight, the entire night club scene, $20,000 worth of scenery and feathered costumes, was scrapped, and replaced by a train interior scene with just two people: the laughter mounted until it became one continuous roar - and the rest is Broadway history.

As Moss Hart himself said "Sometimes play-writing only begins when *End of Act Three* is typed on the manuscript.

Success, however, can sometimes bring its own pressure:

Tim Rice:

Most artists in any field create their best work in the early days of their endeavour: originality and hunger for success are two driving forces of inspiration which inevitably lose their power as time goes by.

Writers become producers: the latter job is crucial to a show's success but is less likely to be the source of something truly barrier-breaking and exciting. Great musicals are 'writer-driven'. After Evita things changed. Never again was I to write a show without an army of experts telling me how to do it. I worried too much about *the rules of the game* and *the critics*.

... and Harold Pinter:

'Success' hasn't changed my writing, but it has made writing more difficult.

I wrote my first three plays quite unselfconsciously in 1957 when the whole world of production was quite remote – I knew they could never be done in the Reps I was acting in, and the West End was on the other side of the moon. Now everything I do seems predictable, unsatisfactory and hopeless. I am a very traditional playwright – for instance I insist on having a curtain in all my plays. I write curtain lines for that reason'.

If you are fortunate enough to have your script accepted, there follows the nightmare of the production period.

John Osborne:

It was frustrating, each week seeming to shorten the breath of what had been brought to life with such difficulty. I was not yet accustomed to the extended period of limbo after a work's exhaustive  struggle to achieve existence, the half-life of anxiety before its lusty proclamation of health and survival in production. These are the playwright's heaviest days, when the play seems poised between life and death.

And the frustration doesn't end with the First Night:

Ken Tynan:

After the Boston opening night of *Picnic* (1953) Joshua Logan (director and co-producer) invited me for a drink in his suite at the Ritz-Carlton. Instead of the quiet chat I was expecting I found S N Behrman in one bedroom, putting laughs into Act One: Tennessee Williams was in another bedroom taking laughs out of Act Two. Asked by Josh 'What's wrong with Act Three?' I said that it somehow seemed to belong to another play. The phone rang. It was Leland Hayward (agent and film producer) calling from California to offer a detailed critique of the Boston opening, totally undeterred by the fact that he had not seen it. Meanwhile a young woman in blue was making some extremely intelligent suggestions for improvements, many of which were subsequently incorporated into the text. Nobody knew who had brought her, and she left without giving her name. I suddenly realised there was one notable absentee.

I asked Josh 'where's the author?' 'Oh, Bill' he said, 'He's in Palm Springs, I think'. The chaos that night taught me more about Broadway than I could have learned in a decade of drama criticism.

The Observer: There is usually a single moment to which a playwright can look back and say *that was when the public accepted me*. For **James Saunders** it may have been the fifteen curtain calls at the West End opening of *A Scent of Flowers*.

The last word on this subject comes from **Noel Coward:**

Consider the public. Treat it with tact and courtesy. It will  accept much from you if you are clever enough to win it to your side. Never fear it nor despise it. Coax it, charm it, interest it, stimulate it, shock it now and then if you must, make it laugh, make it cry, but above all, dear playwrights, never, never, never bore the living hell out of it.

CHAPTER TWENTY-TWO
FINDING MY TAMBOURINE

Some other *tambourine-finders* before I discover my own:-

Kenneth Tynan's Miami Taxi-driver:
Last night's cab-driver told me he came to Miami from New York two years ago and now feels like going back: 'they don't pay enough down here'.
Tonight's cab-driver is a big, moustached man around forty: he also migrated from New York two years ago, and says he wouldn't dream of going back. 'In New York I earned $500 to $1000 dollars a week, I drank too much, I was into drugs, I was miserable. Here I earn $300, I live in the open air, I swim, I sail, I run around the track chasing girls, I'm happy'.
He had found his tambourine.

Victoria Wood:
I had the feeling at University that there was something I could do, but I didn't know what. I lived in a bed-sitter in Birmingham: I was clueless.
I won *New Faces*: nothing.
I appeared on *That's Life*: nothing.
In 1978 I was in a Bush Theatre revue with Julie Walters: I found my voice. It was like banging a gong.
Or a tambourine?

James Agate on Peter Ridgeway.
I am made melancholy by the death of Peter Ridgeway at the age of forty-four. He was the kind of actor who illustrates the strength of weakness. So too did *Charles and Mary*, the play about the Lambs in which he made his reputation. It is a minor miracle that the play ever came to be written, and when written, produced. But the thing happened. For once in a way the key fitted the lock, and this odd, shy little actor, who was reduced to playing stammerers because of ill-health and defective memory, came to personify that other little stammerer, Charles Lamb. His reincarnation of Charles was a miracle of lifelikeness, tenderness, and sensibility.

Now Ridgeway ought never, in this prosaic world, to have been an actor at all. First newsboy, then coffee-shop attendant, he asked and didn't take Matheson Lang's advice, joined an inferior touring company, failed, thought of becoming a monk, joined up in the war, helped at Toc H, studied for the priesthood, learned his job as an actor in Sybil Thorndike's company, started the Players' Theatre in Covent Garden, made and kept it gay, and in the heart of Lamb's own London *was* Charles Lamb. His unremarked career was a tiny edifice of which any stone might at any moment have given way, yet poetic justice arranged that it had its tiny crown, (*found its tambourine*), and was as complete as it ever could have been.

Many of us are subconsciously *searching for our tambourine*, but not everyone will succeed. Finding it is only the end of the beginning: you have to learn to play it – and play it sufficiently well to fill your cap with pennies. Good luck.

Finding my own Tambourine:
I managed a couple of theatres in Scotland and would often be invited to talk to local organisations about the venue's current programme or history. We treated these events as part of our public relations initiative so they usually got a free (or at least a cheap) speaker, and when the word (*cheap!*) got around the number of invitations invariably increased. Offers of return bookings encouraged AROUND THE WORLD IN EIGHTY PLAYS, a new talk encompassing memories and anecdotes from a theatre career which had literally taken me twice around the world, and included eight tours of the Indian sub-continent as well as three long residencies in the Middle East. A more substantial talk and, naturally, at a more substantial fee.

This got me onto the wider Speaker's Circuit, at first mainly the U3As (the University of the Third Age), the Women's Institutes and the Probus Clubs. More return bookings meant more new Talks: one was developed from my experiences touring the Indian sub-continent with British Council drama and dance companies; tours which got me interested in the history of British India. I called the talk WOMEN OF THE RAJ: it highlights both the pleasures and the problems of living in India during the hundred years or so leading up to Independence, and particularly through the period of the Mutiny. It used 'first person' writings from diaries, letters and biographies, material which I had already mined for a full-length play on the same subject LETTERS FROM THE HEN HOUSE, produced at the Byre Theatre in St Andrews in 2006. The new Talk successfully added Ladies Luncheons to my list of engagements.

John Baxter, author of a series of books about Paris, wrote 'the best writing is a mixture of information, reminiscence and personal experience – but that means you have to live your books before you write them'. I believe that applies equally to Talks. My script-writing experience has proved invaluable: a good talk has many of the same qualities as a good play: a narrative with a beginning and an end, with some suspense and the occasional crisis, with light (humour) and dark (poignancy), and – especially important with older audiences - elements of nostalgia. Also, I now realise, an increasing amount of audience involvement (oh, yes there is).

So far, they were straightforward 'talks'; what I called *me and a lectern*, but there was another potential market opening up – the arts centres, the literary festivals – and they would require something bigger, more theatrical. Not quite a complete one-man-show – difficult to fit that into a two-door Vauxhall Corsa - but a presentation using some furniture, or a few props. Possibly a change of jacket. I already knew what my first subject would be: G Bernard Shaw - an 'homage' to the man who (along with Peter O'Toole) had been responsible for my choice of career all those years ago. 'All my life I have been merely playing the clown' he had written, and PLAYING THE CLOWN had to be the title of the presentation: it summed up the man, and hinted that this would not be a dull, academic lecture but a cheerful canter through his personal life and his public works.

PLAYING THE CLOWN appears to start off as a lecture but before long the great man makes his presence felt, correcting me, finishing my lines, taking over the stories – and chatting directly with the audience. It premiered at the Penzance Literary Festival in 2013 and has since taken me (us?) to Scotland, Belfast and France. Sadly, not yet to Dublin,

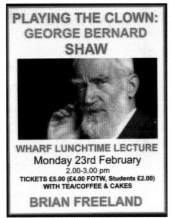

PLAYING THE CLOWN:
GEORGE BERNARD
SHAW

WHARF LUNCHTIME LECTURE
Monday 23rd February
2.00-3.00 pm
TICKETS £5.00 (£4.00 FOTW, Students £2.00)
WITH TEA/COFFEE & CAKES
BRIAN FREELAND

nor to the Shaw Theatre in Canada, but I live in hope. Every performance is a joy, but I particularly remember four. First, the unforgettable experience of introducing Shaw to the France Grande Bretagne Association in a hall on the rue Jeanne d'Arc in Orléans; second, a performance in Ellen Terry's own theatre at Smallhythe (now managed by the National Trust); a presentation in the William Morris Memorial Hall at Kelmscott Manor where Shaw had performed the opening ceremony in 1934: 'I am thrilled to be here and to feel the presence of William Morris' Shaw had said at the time. I, too, was thrilled to be there and to feel the presence of Shaw. The fourth memorable performance was at St John's College as part of the Portsmouth Festivities: a group of the students joined me afterwards wondering why they never saw any of Shaw's plays, and why they weren't told more about this *quite remarkable man*.

My mailing list now includes hundreds of Active Retirement Associations and Retirement Fellowships of various kinds including those run by the NHS and Civil Service. Nostalgia to the fore as I recall my early days at the Palladium, at Butlins, on tour with opera and ballet, all as seen from the stage manager's desk in the prompt corner. THE VIEW FROM THE WINGS is often very different to that of the audience sitting in the stalls or circle especially on those occasions when *everything is not quite alright on the night*.

A slightly saucy talk, and (perhaps for that reason) the most heavily-booked: I have already done it more than one hundred and fifty times, but never get bored with it – it's a beautifully-balanced talk, and tremendous fun.

When I moved down to Sussex I heard that a near-neighbour was John Pick, retired Professor of Arts Administration at City University. I had done the Arts Administration degree course at the Polytechnic of Central London, and using that tenuous link I introduced myself and was invited for coffee. We still enjoy a regular 'cuppa' and some theatre chat, although John is now confined to a wheelchair as a result of complications following hospitalisation with *Guillain Barré Syndrome*.

John passed over to me his entertaining talk THE HISTORY OF EASTBOURNE THEATRES. It is fascinating, but doesn't *travel* so I have broadened it out to 50 YEARS OF SEASIDE ENTERTAINMENT – and in two different versions to satisfy both my 'home territory' in the south-east, and my many bookers in the south-west (I actually do more talks each year in Devon than in Sussex). It includes quite a lot about entertainer Clarkson Rose, whose *Twinkle* summer show operated from 1921 to 1968, including several seasons on Eastbourne Pier until the WW2 bombings forced a move to Torquay, so he nicely straddles both versions of the Talk.

One coffee morning John showed me a paragraph about Clarkson Rose sending a basket of fruit every week to a remand prisoner in Brixton prison. The 'convict' was the notorious Doctor John Bodkins Adams. Clarkie and his partner Olive Fox had settled in Eastbourne where, we discovered, Bodkin Adams was his doctor. Not Olive's: she presumably had heard the rumours about Dr Adams allegedly *easing the passing* of 140 of his elderly (mostly female) patients, and receiving large sums of money and expensive gifts in their wills; gifts which included three Rolls Royce cars. Dr Adams was arrested and tried at the Old Bailey for the murder of just one of the patients, a Mrs Edith Morrell.

I've worked some of this information into the SEASIDE ENTERTAINMENT talk, but the story of the arrest and trial - the longest murder trial of the century at that time (1957) at 17 days - seemed to justify further research, and became the subject of a new musical-comedy (yes, really). Titled SEE YOU IN HEAVEN, it tells the Doctor Adams story within the framework of a Clarkson Rose *Twinkle*-style end-of-pier show with songs and dances and jokes, and several reminders of other entertainers of that period.

The Freelands have tenuous family links with the writer Rudyard Kipling in that one hundred and twenty years before Kipling bought it, Batemans, his lovely Sussex country house and estate now managed by the National Trust was owned by one of my distant ancestors, John Freeland. John was the cousin of my great, great, great grandmother Elizabeth Freeland: the name of my great, great, great grandfather is not recorded and, sadly, this was a not uncommon occurrence in our family tree. John bought Batemans in 1773 for £950, and the purchase documents recorded him as a Salehurst shop-keeper, an occupation unlikely to have provided the wherewithal to buy a country estate so it's interesting to note that at the age of forty, and one year before the purchase, John got married – to a widow, Elizabeth Blunden. I'm guessing a rich widow? Elizabeth's daughter had died after only seven years of marriage, leaving her with two young grand-daughters. They, with John and Elizabeth were the family which moved into Batemans. The father of the two girls, Robert Pattenden, lived on the estate.

Sussex was landfall for both the Romans and the Normans (the Normans actually took over the Roman fort at Pevensey), so the area is rich in history. The iron industry had existed there since pre-Roman times.

In Sussex Parson Levett made cannon; Thomas Brassey (whose ancestors, the de Bercys, had come over with the Conqueror) built railways; Hilaire Belloc (another 'invader' from the continent) became a parliamentarian and prolific author. Their tales fill SUSSEX LIVES: FROM JOHN FREELAND TO RUDYARD KIPLING

Reluctant to be a 'voice from the darkness' I avoided Power-Point presentations for several years but my latest Talks have both been developed from my experiences living and working in France – and really wouldn't work without the pictures. I had written some features about the River Charente for The Scots Thistle magazine, and I returned to the river when preparing my first memoir,  *MEANDERINGS: A RIVER AND A LIFE*. The river is 371 kilometres long with barely 100 metres of straight waterway along the entire length. My theatre career has been similarly *meandering* so the two stories – mine and the river's - are interwoven. Can a river have a story? The Charente certainly has. Henri IV, King of France referred to it as *the most beautiful river in my kingdom* (the projections prove this to be true) but it is so much more: it was the border between the English and the French throughout the three-hundred-years war, and again between the Nazis and the Vichy government in the last war; it was the invasion route for the Vikings; it was the transport route for essentials (salt, food, building materials) and for industrial products (cannon and paper from Angouleme, and cognac from Cognac). It now provides a 371-kilometre-long amenity for boating, swimming, fishing, and generally messing about on the river. All illustrated in

A TRIP DOWN THE RIVER CHARENTE.

With a biography to sell I now have to be available at the end of each talk. Some speakers dislike mixing with the audience afterwards. Here's James Agate:

3.11.1938: 'Lectured in Southport to the members of the St Anne's Women's Luncheon Club. Went well. The worst part of lecturing is afterwards (I see to it that there is no 'before'). When I've given my performance it's over. '*Jetzt hab' ich euch eine Kunst gegeben*' as Wagner said at Bayreuth. I work like a horse to entertain them as an audience: as individuals and total strangers they don't interest me, and I hate being on show. Churlish? Not at all. I just haven't the talent for basking'.

Unlike Agate I treat it as part of the job. Very few people are critical; most want to share common memories of the subject of the talk. Some offer anecdotes. A few even buy my books.

My four-year sojourn in the walled village of Richelieu developed my interest in the man himself; Armand Jean du Plessis, Cardinal Richelieu who – with the King's architect Jacques Lemercier – had designed the *attractive but badly-sited village* built alongside his own Chateau on the family estate between Tours and Poitiers.

When the second son of minor Poitou nobility refused the 'grottiest Bishopric in France', the third son Armand-Jean was proposed as Bishop of Lucon even though at the time he was under the canonical age. As Bishop he became the Almoner to the young Queen Anne of Austria, was sent into exile with the Queen Mother Marie de Medici, and returned to become Cardinal Richelieu, Chief Minister to the young King Louis XIII, and the founder of 'the Nation State of France'.

No photos from that period, of course, but dozens of stunning portraits, paintings and statues by Rubens, Delacroix, Bernini and others: so stunning that the Powerpoint Presentation RICHELIEU: THE CARDINAL AND HIS CITÉ has at last gained me access to the huge Arts Society circuit. Previously, they had considered my Talks *not sufficiently 'arty'*. O wad some power the gift gie us to see ourselves as ithers see us.

With this series of solo performances and presentations, a portfolio of scripts for both stage and screen, and an almost-sold-out memoir I feel that the experiences of the previous sixty years in and around the theatre have all come together. The writing, the production, the direction, the design, the stage management, the lighting, the administration, the publicity – all are as essential to a one-man-show as to a major opera company.

To his encyclopaedic treatise *The Seven Ages of Theatre* Richard Southern added a footnote: 'One irregularity of theatrical presentation seems to transcend classification: this is the single player – the performer who carries his whole show on his own personality'.

Over recent years I have sensed the development of a *presenter's persona*: I am now more comfortable among strangers, less of a *loner*, even beginning to *like* myself. Thanks to this strange combination of experiences (I remain too modest to claim 'talents') this *outsider's* retirement is busy and, more importantly, is both enjoyable and satisfying. I have a reason to get out of bed every morning: like Frank Field 'I love every day, and that is a privilege compared to people who work in a job they loathe'. I have found *my* tambourine.

Now, where did I put my cap?

CHAPTER TWENTY-THREE
CURTAIN CALLS

Franco Zeffirelli:

Just as I was about to deliver this text to the printer the radio announced the death of Franco Zeffirelli at the age of 96. He described his own style as lavish in scale and unashamedly theatrical, and one cannot argue with that. He benefited greatly from his (self-engineered) relationship with Visconti, although the resulting work opportunities and personal contacts with such as Coco Chanel, Anna Magnani and Maria Callas succeeded through his own charm and talents as much as any influence from Visconti – and he actually became involved in opera (designing *The Italian Girl in Algiers* at La Scala) before Visconti himself.

'Luchino showed me the world of creativity in theatre and films, how to conceive an idea and how to bring together a whole world of culture that could embody it. In other words, how to direct'. Covent Garden invited him to direct the double bill of *Cavalleria Rusticana* and *I Pagliacci*, and that success led Michael Benthal to invite Zeffirelli to direct an Italian-style *Romeo and Juliet* at the Old Vic. Later, he returned to the Old Vic for the National Theatre's *Much Ado*. Although less in need of a *tambourine* than we ordinary practitioners he nevertheless found it with his film productions of the later Verdi operas, *La Traviata* and *Otello*. 'I enjoy my life wholeheartedly; I am not tortured by self-doubt or driven by creative *angst*. I rather like being famous. I know I ought to pretend that it's a bore being recognised in the street and being asked for my autograph, but it isn't. It's rather pleasant'. *Requiescat in Pace*, Franco.

John Dyer:

A little rule, a little sway,
A sunbeam on a winter's day,
Is all the proud and mighty have
Betwixt the cradle and the grave.

I forgot to tell you about the cat:
Back in the introduction I mentioned that we 'acquired a cat'.
On our way to the get-rid-of-the-dinars supper in Yugoslavia
we had heard vague miaows in the bushes: on the way back
the miaows continued so we searched the bushes and
discovered a tiny black kitten, one front leg hanging
uselessly. Being British we naturally took it back to the bus
where the girls cleaned it up and fed it. We named the new
crew member Doris.

She travelled quite happily on the 'navigator's table' beside
the driver. I hung a ball from the roof, and Doris would lie on
her back playing with it: three legs at first, and then four as
the other one got stronger. Strong enough for her to leap out
of the bus at every stop. Sadly not every stop was a camp site
and, one day, in Crete, she shot out under the wheels of a
passing truck. Mary sent us a card 'Alas, poor Doris'.

James Agate on Ellen Terry:
Ellen Terry, at the Gaiety Theatre, Manchester, playing Alice
Sit-by-the-Fire on the night after Sir Henry Irving died. Just
before the end Alice says 'It's summer done, autumn begun.
Farewell summer. The moon is full tonight, Robert, but it
isn't looking for me any more. Taxis farewell – advance four-
wheelers, I had a beautiful husband once, black as the raven
was his hair' . . . Here Ellen broke down utterly. The curtain
fell in silence, and we all left the theatre quietly, feeling that
we had intruded on a private sorrow.

Sir Ralph Richardson:
I have never been particularly afraid of dying. I'm amazed
that I'm as old as I am. I always had the idea that when I was
old I would get frightfully clever. I'd get awfully learned, get
jolly sage. People would come to me for advice. But nobody
ever comes to me for anything, and I don't know a thing.

Kenneth Tynan remembered Richardson as the dying Cyrano,
sitting in a convent garden with autumn leaves twirling and
floating about him. 'Even then he looked odd, absent-minded,
solitary, absurd, noble and desolate'.

Agate thought Richardson's Falstaff *something better than virtuosity in character acting*. 'Peace, good Doll. Do not speak like a death's head. Do not bid me remember mine end'.

Lilian Baylis:
After the funeral her body was taken first to the Old Vic, where a loving crowd was waiting to pay homage to the passing of its queen, then on to the Sadlers Wells Opera House, and finally to Golders Green Crematorium where the last rites were taken by her old friend Father Andrew of the Society of the Divine Compassion.
'God gave Lilian Baylis the vocation to be the mother and mistress of her theatres and their companies. They were the complete devotion and sincerity of her life'.

Celia Johnson:
I was watching a rehearsal of *Hay Fever* when Celia came and sat beside me. As we watched Dame Edith Evans on stage Celia suddenly whispered 'Oh I do wish they would let me understudy her'. Of course the whole idea was preposterous, a star of Celia's magnitude understudying anyone, even Dame Edith, but in the next coffee break I passed on her thoughts to the director/playwright Sir Noel Coward. Celia not only covered for Dame Edith, but took over the role later in the run and was perfect. Celia once said, at another star's crowded memorial service 'there won't be so many when I go; you'll have to paper the house'. Eventually, when that sad day came, I was at *her* memorial service, and it was standing room only.

Roy Castle:
Looking back on my career, I have made so many mistakes and shudder to think how I could have been so stupid so often. This, then, raises the question 'What do you want out of life? What is success?' The answers are much clearer once you are told life's just about over. The simple, loving, caring things then score heavily, and the greed, selfishness and ego become millstones.

Die? That's the Last Thing I'll Do.
(part of an article which first appeared in the Scots Thistle Magazine in 2008)

With Easter following just a few days after my seventieth birthday I hope I can be excused if my thoughts keep turning towards mortality. Not in any morbid way: my father was an undertaker, and for many years his mortuary was in a room of our home. It had its own outside door, so the corpses didn't actually enter from the street, through the front door with its coloured-glass window, passing the front room where the best china was displayed in glass-fronted cabinets and a dusty piano waited for Auntie Nell to bring it back to life at the next very-occasional family gathering.
Death, like love, was 'all around', a part of our everyday life. Indeed, it paid the bills, and made our life possible, so we youngsters had a healthy respect for, and an unhealthy interest in, Dad's work.

During Dad's year as President of the British Institute of Embalmers he was invited to audition for the television programme *What's My Line* – his only connection with show business, as far as I know. Wisely, they didn't use him. His respect for his profession, and for his 'clientele', would not have allowed him to develop the humorous potentialities needed for a light entertainment programme.

Not that undertakers are without humour: 'It's a dead end job, but it's a living' they will cheerfully tell you as they set off to work at the 'dead centre of the town'. His proudest moment, I believe, was when he was 'conducting' a big funeral – hearse and four cars –crossing Hammersmith Broadway in the rush hour. Solid traffic in every direction. He put on his top hat, held his rolled umbrella aloft and, walking in front of the hearse, cleared a way through the crush. One would have to be madder than King Lear to attempt such a feat today, but that was back in the days when we stood silently and took off our hats when a funeral cortège passed by.

A Sequel: Ten Years Later.
What, still here?

With Easter following just a few days after my *eightieth* birthday and every third thought turning towards my grave, I wondered if those thoughts might contribute towards the anticipated funeral expenses as the subject of a script. A comedy about death, perhaps? Not *my* death, naturally; that's no laughing matter. So whose, then?

During the previous years I had spent more time and effort than was justified in attempts to adapt a friend's novel into, first, a stage play, and then into a film script. The friend is

that renowned Scottish author Christopher Rush. We first met in 1986 when his moving evocation of childhood in a Fife fishing village *A Twelvemonth and a Day* was turned into an equally-moving film *Venus Peter* by producer Christopher Young. As Director of Fife's only Regional Film Theatre I was determined to get a preview screening before its official opening: I actually got much more, as the two Christophers turned up to answer questions after the screening.

Chris Rush and I turned the book into a stage epic which was premiered (with the generous support of the Scottish Arts Council) by the enterprising Dollar Drama Group. We later adapted one of his short stories, *Lilies That Fester*, into a one-act play which won the Benedetti Salver in the Scottish Community Drama Association annual competition, and picked up a Geoffrey Whitworth award as one of the top six New British One Act Plays of 2006.

When Ben Kingsley and Kevin Spacey started bidding for  performance rights to *Will*, Christopher's 496-page fictitious biography of William Shakespeare, Chris wondered if we might attempt a screenplay. The obvious answer was 'no'. For 496 pages two elderly men, the dying Shakespeare and his lawyer Francis Collins, discuss last-minute changes to the playwright's 'will' and reminisce about the past. Very little action, and absolutely no *crisis* (which, we argued earlier, is one probable essence of drama).

Kingsley's bid wins, but he can't get a script (surprise, surprise). He hangs on to the film rights, and Spacey snaps up the stage rights for the Old Vic Theatre (where, to his eternal credit, his experience, talent and energy secured the future of that venerable institution). Chris is immediately on the phone: can we do a stage script? I should have said 'no', but I'm more at home in a theatre so I read the 496 pages for the fifth time, gave it a go, and sent the finished script off to Spacey. I'm not embarrassed by the result, but I'd had to 'open up' the book to make it more 'theatrical', and guessed that it would be too big for Sir Kevin's budget. A few months later he announced the end of his Old Vic tenure. The script was not returned. Sad to say, they very rarely are although we writers conscientiously enclose an SAE. I'm convinced that the National and the RSC use the SAEs for their own outgoing mail. I absolve two men from this criticism: Sir Cameron Mackintosh and Sir Nicholas Hytner both enclosed polite, helpful – and signed – notes with the returned scripts. However, before you flood their mail boxes with your latest scribbles I should add that they have never accepted an unsolicited script, and their programming policies suggest that they never will.

Chris is on the phone again: another management has bought the film rights. Can we.....? By this time I had actually just completed my first screenplay, *Fruits de Mer*, an adaptation of two Emile Zola short stories.

This encouraged me to read those 496 pages for the sixth and seventh and – I hope – last time. I have probably read *Will* more times than anyone else in the world: it is a tremendous literary achievement but not without faults. However, this time I was consciously seeking alternatives to the weaker scenes and - I believe – finding them. So we now have both a stage script and a screenplay, neither of which are likely to be taken up.

Several (unpaid) months of my fast-ebbing life wasted on Rush/Shakespeare adaptations and – wait a minute – an idea. Somewhere I had read of a note in a Stratford vicar's diary of an evening when Will Shakespeare, Ben Jonson and Michael Drayton enjoyed a *Merry Meeting* in the Bell Inn at Welford a few days prior to Shakespeare's death – a death supposedly caused by a chill caught riding home in the rain from that same meeting. We had this strong Shakespeare character from Christopher's book, and already a great mass of relevant theatrical and cinematic material. Could we not use some of this to bring that evening at the Bell Inn to life? We could; we did; and we now have a comedy about the death of Shakespeare. Title is *A Merry Meeting*. Seven characters, single set. All we need now is a room above a pub somewhere. . . .

Shakespeare: (who died at 52)
Goodnight sweet prince, and flights of angels sing thee to thy rest.

Hazlitt: (who also died at 52)
I have loitered my life away, reading books, looking at pictures, going to plays, thinking, writing on what pleased me best. I have wanted only one thing to make me happy (*a tambourine?*) but, wanting that, have wanted everything.
In the outset of life our imagination has a body to it. As we advance, we exhaust our fund of enjoyment and of hope. As we taste the pleasures of life, their spirit evaporates, the sense palls; and nothing is left but the phantoms, the lifeless shadows of what has been!

Concert Party's Days are Over . . .

They had started with the Minstrels
In black faces, on the shore.
Performing in all weathers,
Three times daily, sometimes more.
Pennies in the bottle from the punters on the benches
Till the punters and performers all departed for the trenches.
Their banjos joined the other instruments of war;
Now kids play on Bouncy Castles
Where the Minstrels played before.

Following the Minstrels came a little Pierrot Show
In a rusty pier-end theatre with roaring waves below.
Although the finances were tight,
The six of them, in black and white,
Braving the theatre's pale gaslight,
They did their best to 'keep it bright' –
But now there's television, and a tea-tray on your knee,
And supermarkets trading where the theatres used to be.

Concert Party's days are over;
No more contracts to fulfil.
No more cheery end-of-pier shows;
No more packed variety bills.
No more early morning calls,
No cheering stalls in music halls;
No more band calls, rehearsal calls,
And worst of all – no Curtain Calls.
Just a hamper full of costumes from our summers by the sea
And a big empty hole where the magic used to be.

George Bernard Shaw on the death of his wife:
Charlotte died last Sunday, 12th September 1943, at half past
two in the morning. Since 1939 she suffered much pain, and
lately some distress from hallucinations of crowds of people
in her room. Her disease, a horror called *osteitis deformans*
which bent and furrowed her into a Macbeth witch (albeit an
amiable one), was progressing steadily and incurably, but last
Friday a miracle occurred.

She suddenly threw off her years, her visions, her furrows,
her distresses, and had thirty hours of youth and happiness
before the little breath she could draw failed. By morning she
looked twenty years younger. It was a blessedly happy
ending, and a deeply moving one.

At Charlotte's funeral, music from Handel's *Messiah*
accompanied the committal, and Shaw, my companion
throughout this book, lifted up his arms and sang softly as the
coffin moved away.
Shaw was a vegetarian: 'Animals are my friends and I don't
eat my friends. At my funeral there won't be any people, just
all the animals I haven't eaten'.

Hazlitt: On the Fear of Death
The pleasures of our existence have worn themselves out, are
'gone into the wastes of time' or have turned their indifferent
side to us: the pains of their repeated blows have worn us out,
and have left us neither spirit nor inclination to encounter
them again in retrospect. We do not want to rip up old
grievances, nor to renew our youth like the phoenix, nor to
live our lives twice over. Once is enough. As the tree falls, so
let it lie.

Lytton Strachey - on his deathbed:
If this is it, I don't think much of it.

Hazlitt:
We shut up the book and close the account once and for all.

BIBLIOGRAPHY:

Special Thanks to:
Wikipedia
Google/Google Images
Jagath Kosmodara for the front cover picture
Mac McNamee for the back cover photo
and G Bernard Shaw for his company along the way.

Grateful Thanks to:
Agate, James: Those Were The Nights, Hutchinson 1946
Agate, James: My Theatre Talks, Barker 1933
Allen, John: History of Theatre in Europe. Heinemann 1983
Archer, William: Play-Making, Pantianos Classics 1912
Archer & Lowe (Eds.): Hazlitt on Theatre, Walter Scott Ltd 1895
Artaud/Corti: The Theatre & Its Double, Alma Classics 1964
Bablet, Denis: Theatre of Edward Gordon Craig, Eyre Methuen.
Barrault, Jean-Louis: Reflections on Theatre, Rockliff Publishing
Bentley, Eric: In Search of Theatre, Applause Theatre Books
Bentley, Eric: What is Theatre? Methuen 1944
Billington, Michael: Stoppard, the Playwright, Methuen 1987
Bingham, Madeleine: Irving, George Allen & Unwin
Blakemore, Michael: Stage Blood, Faber & Faber 2013
Brook, Peter: The Empty Space, McGibbon & Kee 1968
Brown, Frederick: Culture of the French Stage, Viking Press 1980
Craig, Edward: Edward Gordon Craig, Limelight Editions 1985
Craig, E G: On The Art of Theatre, Browns Bookstore, Chicago
Croall, Jonathan: The Coming of Godot, Oberon Books 2005
Croall, Jonathan: Closely Observed Theatre, Fantom Films 2014
Daubeny, Peter: My World of Theatre, Jonathan Cape 1971
Dukes, Ashley: Drama, OUP 1947
Dukes, Ashley: The Scene is Changed, Macmillan 1942
Eyre, Richard: National Service, Bloomsbury 2003/4
Eyre, Richard: Talking Theatre, Nick Hern Books 2009
Eyre, Richard: People, Politics and Arts, Nick Hern Books 2014
Fagg, Edwin: The Old Old Vic, Vic-Wells Ass'n 1936
Findlater, Richard: Lilian Baylis, Allen Lane 1975
Freeland, Brian: Meanderings: A River and a Life: ATWP 2017
Gaskill, William: A Sense of Direction, Faber & Faber 1988
Goodie, Sheila: Annie Horniman, Methuen 1990
Goodwin, John (Ed.): RSC 1960-63, Max Reinhardt Ltd 1964
Granville-Barker, Harley: On Dramatic Method, Hill&Wang NY.
Granville-Barker: The Exemplary Theatre, Little, Brown. 1922
Granville-Barker, Harley: Selected Essays, Bloomsbury 2017
Hardwick, Cedric: A Victorian In Orbit, Methuen 1961
Hart, Moss: Act One, An Autobiography,St Martins Griffin, NY
Hartnoll, Phyllis: Concise History of Theatre, Thames & Hudson

Hazlitt, William: Selected Writings, Penguin 1985
Hobson, Harold: Theatre, Burke 1953
Hobson, Harold: Theatre in Britain, Phaidon 1984
Holroyd, Michael: Bernard Shaw (3 vols) Chatto & Windus 1991
Holroyd, Michael: A Strange Eventful History, Chatto & Windus
Kapoor, Shashi: The Prithviwallahs, Roli Books
Kendal, Felicity: White Cargo, Michael Joseph 1998
Kendal, Geoffrey: Shakespeare Wallah, Penguin 1987
Kiernander, Adrian: Ariane Mnouchkine, CUP.
Leeper, Janet: E G Craig, Theatre Designs, King Penguin, 1948
Marowitz & Trussler (Eds): Theatre at Work, Methuen 1967
McCarthy, Lillah: Myself & My Friends, E P Dutton 1933
Melvin, Murray (Ed.): The Art of Theatre Workshop, Oberon
Miller, Jonathan: Subsequent Performances, Faber & Faber 1986
Mongredien, Geo: Life in French Theatre, George Allen & Unwin
Monro, C K: Watching a Play, Gerald Howe Ltd 1931
Priestley, J B: The Art of the Dramatist, Heinemann 1957
Purdom, C B (Ed.): The Shaw-Barker Letters, Phoenix House
Robertson, Graham W: Time Was, Hamish Hamilton 1931
Rose, Clarkson: With a Twinkle in my Eye, Museum Press 1951
Rudlin, John: Jacques Copeau, Cambridge University Press
Southern, Richard: Seven Ages of the Theatre, Faber & Faber
Speaight, Robert: William Poel, Heinemann 1954
Taylor, John Russell, Rise/Fall of the Well-Made Play, Methuen
Thorndike, Sybil and Russell: Lilian Baylis. Chapman & Hall '38
Wardle, Irving: Theatres of George Devine, Jonathan Cape. 1978
Wells & Stanton (Eds): Shakespeare On Stage. CUP. 2002
Williams, Harcourt (Ed): Work of Lilian Baylis, Shenval Press
Wilson, Colin: The Outsider, Victor Gollanz Lyd 1956
Zeffirelli, Franco: The Autobiography, Weidenfeld and Nicholson

Special Mentions to:
Sir Richard Eyre
Peter Gill
Mary G Evans
Khalid Tyabji
Mike Strudwick
V&A Images.

INDEX:

My thanks to Jagath for permission to use his *Tambourine Player* on the front cover. This is one of his series of paintings of the annual Perahera at Kandy, the Procession of the Sacred Tooth, one of the biggest events in the Sri Lankan calendar.

JAGATH KOSMODARA

Jagath Kosmodara's career as an artist and celebrated comic illustrator began in 1981. His work has been featured in numerous Sri Lankan newspapers, and internationally in Amazon.com publications such as Mom's Surprise and Brer Anancy and Brer Duck. His three exhibitions in Sri Lanka have been widely acclaimed by the local connoisseurs, with the most recent, 'Thambasancharaya (Journey of Copper Sand)' receiving rave reviews.

He is in addition a veteran of the Sri Lankan and Dubai advertising industry having served at institutions such as J. Walter Thompson and Mullen Lowe for 35 years.

Jagath Kosmodara is represented by Ashraff Associates.
info@ashraffassociates.com

**For more information about any of the
Books, Scripts, Talks or Presentations
mentioned in the text, please see the website
www.brianfreeland.co.uk**